PAKISTAN, ISLAM, AND ECONOMICS

FAILURE OF MODERNITY

PAKISTAN, ISLAM, AND ECONOMICS
FAILURE OF MODERNITY

Izzud-Din Pal

OXFORD
UNIVERSITY PRESS

OXFORD

UNIVERSITY PRESS

Great Clarendon Street, Oxford OX2 6DP

Oxford University Press is a department of the University of Oxford.
It furthers the University's objective of excellence in research, scholarship,
and education by publishing worldwide in

Oxford New York

Athens Auckland Bangkok Bogotá Buenos Aires Calcutta
Cape Town Chennai Dar es Salaam Delhi Florence Hong Kong Istanbul
Karachi Kuala Lumpur Madrid Melbourne Mexico City Mumbai
Nairobi Paris São Paulo Singapore Taipei Tokyo Toronto Warsaw

with associated companies in Berlin Ibadan

Oxford is a registered trade mark of Oxford University Press
in the UK and in certain other countries

ISBN 0 19 579068 5

Printed in Pakistan at
Al-Rehman Paper Craft, Karachi.
Published by
Ameena Saiyid, Oxford University Press
5-Bangalore Town, Sharae Faisal
PO Box 13033, Karachi-75350, Pakistan.

To the Memory of My Mother

Contents

Preface

This book offers a critical examination of the Islamic economic system, as defined by the traditionalist ulama. It is the result of ten years of study and reflection on the subject that straddles many disciplines. My approach, therefore, is necessarily eclectic. My main objective is to address the informed reader. I have added explanatory notes in parentheses in the text wherever technical jargon has been used.

In my interpretation of the issues examined in the book, I have taken advantage of the primary as well as the secondary sources, both in English and Urdu languages. The debt of gratitude that I owe in developing my understanding of the subject goes beyond what is reflected in my bibliography. I have learnt a great deal from my contacts with the other economists in the field as well as specialists in the Islamic literature, extending over a period of many years, often absorbing ideas, not always remembering their source.

Three institutions are considered essential to establish the Islamic economic system: the elimination of *riba*, the implementation of the laws of inheritance, and the organization of *zakat*. The central point of Islamicization in Pakistan, however, has been on the issue of *riba*. No similar zeal has been shown by the proponents of Islamicization for an assessment of the workings of the laws of inheritance, or about the perceived or real problems relating to *zakat*. The obsessive focus on the reward to capital is not matched by a regard for fair compensation which ought to be earned by labour. Concerning the question wages in urban areas, for example, it is explained away by means of platitudes. In agriculture, the bias is clearly in favour of the landlord. This imbalance raises interesting questions, and establishes flaccid foundation for the development of the proposed new Islamic economic order. As I point out in the book, the imbalance to a degree stems from the emphasis which is put solely on the Islamic ideal, as defined by the Islamicists, against the Western reality. The question of *riba* lends itself to such an approach. The other two institutions would require a discussion of the Muslim reality, which is considered irrelevant for the *homo Islamicus* (the model pious Muslim).

The Islamicists in Pakistan define the concept of *riba* in a very narrow and a rigid manner, and they expect that the entire economic system would be changed to correspond with their criterion. Their position is completely out of line in the context of the Muslim world as a whole. Two Muslim countries, for example, claim to have established an Islamic economic order, Sudan and Iran. Perhaps one could find a strong trend of orthodoxy in Sudan, but to examine that country's political economy would not be a worthwhile exercise from the point of view of Pakistan. The case of Iran is more complex and also quite distinct from what the Pakistani Islamicists advocate. In the first place, the nuances of the Shia doctrine and the role of the ulama in that society present a very different perspective from that of Pakistan. Secondly, the credit policies of the banks in Iran are intertwined with the economic policies of the government in various spheres of the economy, and payment of amount in excess of the principal on government borrowings is not considered *riba*. Also, regulation of minimum and maximum rates of return on various financial activities are strictly followed, and the role of intermediation by banks is mainly between the savers and the investors, and they do not engage in usual commercial activities. They impose service charges on a percentage basis, which is considered *riba* by the Pakistani Islamicists. The Iranian position on the justification of rate of interest to accommodate the eroding effect of inflation is quite flexible.

To examine all these questions with reference to Iran would be a very useful exercise. It would, however, constitute a major enterprise and must be left for another opportunity.

In other Muslim countries, the Islamic banks operate side by side the traditional banks. The political elite in these countries make periodic pronouncements to establish the Islamic economic order; still in other countries, including Saudi Arabia, the dichotomy between the sharia law and the economic fact is conveniently ignored.

A small group of implacable and distinctly tendentious proponents of interest-free economy exists in Pakistan, and it seems to have a receptive audience in selected groups. How does one explain this phenomenon? Perhaps it is possible to seek an answer in the socio-political framework of the country. There is, for example, a sharp inequality of incomes among the people and it is reflected in the banking system. The common man does not have the means to make use of this institution. In the middle income range, a vast majority tend to hold small deposits, and the top-ranking depositors are in a minority. The loans and advances, on the other hand, are almost exclusively the privilege of the upper classes, and this creates a secondary effect on transfer of income in their favour. Given this fact, and owing to what I refer to in the book as the soft-state syndrome, the principle of profit-sharing, with the expectation of avoiding losses, would be eminently suitable to this class.

My contention is further reinforced by the gap between the theory and praxis, which produces suitable conditions for the use of devices to cover the existing practice under a new name. Also, as I suggest in the book, the ruling classes would be inclined to adopt these reforms if only to divert attention away from the real economic problems facing the country, by taking refuge in the 'transitional' situation created as a result of these measures.

I should add that in Islamic jurisprudence, one can find both the conservative and quite radical positions about the role of labour in the economy. This is an important question and I have not included it in the book; it deserves a separate examination, as an exercise in Islamic thought.

The irony is that in the current debate on the *riba*-fee economy the main issue has been pushed aside. The classical jurists, in defining *riba*, have established the criterion that an individual owner of capital is entitle to receive reward for use of his capital *only when he participates in the risk of the enterprise*, and that his risk must be clearly *identifiable*. All four schools of jurisprudence in the Sunni tradition emphasize this principle. Abu Hanifa, with his pragmatic approach, however, accepted as legitimate several departures from this rule in the context of the needs of business. In modern times, as I argue in the book, this *identifiability* has completely disappeared, whether the source of income for the owner of capital is *modaraba* certificate or the bank PLS (Profit-and-loss sharing). This criterion becomes further diluted in suggestions for Islamic modes in order to replace the existing instruments used in government financing , and this is the main reason why I have ignored this subject in the book. The distinction between the Islamic financial system and the traditional financial system, therefore, has become a matter of semantics. The underlying theme in the Islamic system turns out to be a form of equity capital, without all the regulations which are associated with the modes of financing such as mutual funds and other cooperative or adventure forms of investment in the developed countries. It also needs to be noted that in spite of legal and customary safeguards, the Western financial system is subjected to constant scrutiny in the open societies.

The historical question whether Pakistan was to be an Islamic state or a Muslim country remains of paramount importance in the framework of my book. It is a controversial issue among historians. As mentioned in the

book, the direct evidence about the views of the Muslim
League leadership on the question of identity of Pakistan is
lacking and, therefore, one has to speculate and use
subjective judgement. I have been guided by my
impressions on the matter, which I gathered in the
formative years as a college student in Amritsar. I took
active part in the Pakistan movement through my affiliation
with the Punjab Muslim Students Federation during 1942–
7. In later years, I have made an effort to examine the
historical literature related to the period including memoirs
and personal accounts of some leaders of he Muslim
League in order to refresh my perspective on the subject. I
have found no reason to change my views.

Pakistan was not a social movement in the ordinary sense
of the term. The main focus of Mr Jinnah was to protect
the national interests of Muslims in any future
constitutional arrangement for British India from the thick
shadow of Hindu dominance. That is what attracted the
Muslim mind and became a mass movement. There was
considerable evidence from the history of Hindu-Muslim
relations, and especially from the experience of provincial
rule under the 1935 constitutional reforms, that a working
rapprochement between the two communities was becoming
difficult. In the leadership of the Indian National Congress,
those who accused Muslim League of being a communal
organization were in fact themselves committed to the goal
of Hindutva.

The main objective of the Pakistan movement was to
liberate the prevalent political structure in the Muslim
majority areas from the Indian centre after the British rule.
No drastic change in this structure was anticipated. This is
an entirely different approach from building up an
organization for establishing an ideological state. There
were suggestions made from time to time that the 1940
Resolution , later known as the Pakistan Resolution, would
open up the opportunity for a *khilafat* for Muslims. The
leaders of the Muslim league, especially Mr Jinnah,

scrupulously avoided any association with such an idea. I believe that the concept of the Islamic state, which was germinated through the Objectives Resolution of 1949, reinforced by the 1973 Constitution under Zulfikar Ali Bhutto and made popular, especially during and since the period of General Ziaul Haq, is a later innovation.

What would be involved in the new political freedom for Muslims? There was no official grand design for the new country. A likely scenario would have been to have Muslims discuss and debate issues of immediate concern as well as matters relating to long term policies, and arrive at decisions in light of the principles enunciated by Islam. The Muslim civic order would have the opportunity to consolidate and expand in the new setting. I never thought, however, that attempts would be made to introduce Islamization by fiat. Nor did I ever think that some members of the intelligentsia who made claims to cherish freedom and democracy would be willing to fervently serve a military dictator.

The fact, however, is that while the politicians have been vigorously promoting the idea of the Islamic state, the civil order is in serious decline. The intellectual life of the nation in spite of its occasional flashes has really not prospered. The atmosphere seems to be unfavorable of pure research and hostile to debate and controversy. With all the emphasis on the Islamics system, no major work had been produced in Pakistan in recent years on the interpretation of Islam in modern times, with the notable exception of the book by Khalifa Abdul Hakim.

The political system inherited from British India seems to have brought with it an insidious colonial culture, an archaic remnant from the old days of the Raj. The *chaprasi* and the driver are important symbols of this life style. They perform a useful function at the bottom of the hierarchy, without any distinction between what belongs to the domestic sphere and what is rightfully the office duty, and of course their working day cannot easily be measured in the usual jargon. The bureaucracy, the governorships, the presidency, the legislative and municipal bodies, and judiciary all seem to have the same pattern of relationship among them which was created by the British rulers of India to meet their needs. The legal system in large part is the same as in the colonial period and the acts, rules and ordinances are enforced as 'adapted' for Pakistan. And there has not been a significant change in the role assigned to the machinery of law and order, which is essentially based on master-subject approach to governance.

Pakistan came into being, then, as a result of the exclusive attention given to the constitutional solution to Indian independence. Perhaps Quaid-i-Azam Mohammad Ali Jinnah could have made an effort to anticipate events beyond his horizon. Perhaps, also, through some inexplicable historical accident, a statesman or statesmen, might have emerged from the new political class in the new country, especially in the Punjab. The first question cannot, in my view, be answered until the second is carefully examined. The relations between the centre and East Pakistan, as it was known, are gradually being documented. Not much work has been done on the politics of the centre vis á vis the other provinces from an historical point of view. The period from 1949 to the 'Punjab Disturbances of 1953' remains, for example, to be critically scrutinized. I believe that it was an important turning point for Pakistan. A Machiavellian game was played behind the facade of a religious issue, which should have been settled through an open debate. With the passage of time, as new problems have emerged, the challenge to resolve these problems has remained firmly grounded in the rules of the game established during that period.

It seems to me that the first question concerning the political legacy of the Quaid-i-Azam becomes just an academic exercise, in light of the above issues, which remain unresolved.

The book would not have been possible without the help, which I received from friends in Pakistan, and who gave me all the necessary assistance in making contacts and in getting relevant information I needed in my work. In Montréal, the library of the Institute of Islamic Studies of McGill University has been within easy reach for all the necessary references that I needed for my work. At the Centre for Developing-Area Studies, also of McGill University, the librarian, Mr Iain Blair, has helped me beyond the call of his duty, often alerting me about the latest acquisitions related to my subject. It is a pleasure for me to acknowledge the support that I have received from my daughters, Mariam and Salma, throughout these years, especially since the death of their mother. Salma has made an additional contribution by assisting me in the preparation of the index.

A brief comment on the methodology is in order. I followed the Oxford Dictionary and Oxford Writers' Dictionary for guidance in spelling of words, with a few exceptions in which I accommodated the customary usage. I have not followed the rules of transliteration of the Arabic-Persian-Urdu words and of proper names used in the book. There are many forms and practices in vogue in the South Asian literature on religion and politics. I have stayed on a middle course and tried to maintain uniformity throughout the book. I have, for example, used Qur'an, not Koran; ulama, not ulema; Syed Ahmad Khan, not Sayyed Ahmad Khan, *sharia*, not *shariah* or *shariat*, *sunna*, not sunnah or sunnat.

I should offer an explanation for using the word 'Islamicization' and not 'Islamization' in the book. I believe that 'Islamization' is a broad term which underlines the important aspect of Islam: the submission to the Will of God. The contemporary traditionalist Muslims do not have an exclusive claim to interpret Islam. Some writers describe these proponents of Islamic order as *Islamiyun*. I prefer to call them Islamicists. The adjective 'Islamic' defines their specific objectives. What criteria they use to establish their agenda to Islamicize the economy by means of selective use of Islamic jurisprudence, then, becomes an important issue.

The recent move to strengthen the role of the *sharia* by means of the Fifteenth Amendment, came to late to be included in the book. It is, however, a proposal that, as I suggest in the book with reference to the discussion of the Sharia Act of 1991, could have been anticipated. There is a notable difference, however. If the government is to be empowered to give *directions* to Muslim about what is good and what is evil in the conduct of their lives, then a question arises about the nature of the government itself. Can a prime minister, who has no religious standing of any kind, and who is under the penumbra of accusations about his financial affairs, be allowed to perform this responsibility? Throughout the various general elections held in Pakistan, the religious parties were never able to gain much power. Now there would be an opening available to them, irrespective of the fate of this bill. The spirit of the Ash'arite philosophy promoted by Abul A'la Maudoodi continues to haunt Pakistan.

Chapter 1 is from an article which originally appeared in the *Journal of Contemporary Asia*, under the same title as this book. Chapters 3 and 7 are based on a revision of two articles, which were published in the *Middle Eastern Studies*. The permission to include these articles in the book is grateful acknowledged.

The book is dedicated to the memory of my mother. My father would have wholeheartedly approved of this decision, had he been alive.

Montréal   Izzud-Din Pal
30 October 1998

Introduction

This book is about religious thought in Islam, from the point of view of an economist. The continuing ideological push for establishing a truly Islamic state in Pakistan raises the question about reinterpretation of the Qur'anic moral pronouncements and injunctions. This issue is not unique to Pakistan, except that unlike other Muslim countries, this country was carved out of British India on the basis of religious identity. I do not intend to compare the development of Islamic thought and practice on economic issues in Pakistan with other Muslim countries. It would be beyond the scope of this study. Also, the Islamic outlook and tradition in India-Pakistan were conditioned by the place of Muslims in the framework of the history of the subcontinent: after having been a ruling minority in the region, in search of their identity since the Revolt of 1857. Nevertheless, the analysis presented here has wider relevance for all Muslim communities, which are united on the sacred role of the Qur'an and the Holy Prophet in their lives.

My focus is on the juristic arguments and on a modernist perspective on these arguments, I use the word 'modernist' in a broad sense to include all those who believe that the laws and institutions developed during the medieval period of Islam are not immutable. It means, more specifically, Islamic modernism which embraces to those Muslims who believe that the Qur'anic verses should be examined in the context of the social framework in which they were revealed and their message reconstructed in the light of modern times. Professor Fazlur Rahman is a distinguished example of an Islamic modernist. The secular-minded Muslims may also be called modernists, albeit on the other end of the spectrum. In fact their position on the future of Islam as religion would not be as diametrically opposed to the former group, as might appear, because they too would favour a re-examination of the classical jurisprudence, but would keep religion out of politics, on the assumption that religious and ethical values should be reflected in personal behaviour, to provide guidance in political decision-making process and to serve as an inspiration in daily life. Modernism, whether of the first or the second variety has a very fragile place in Islamic thought, because the mainstream literature is dominated by the pharisaic Islam of the ulama. With reference to the four schools of Islamic jurisprudence in the Sunni tradition, the consensus of opinions in these schools as interpreted by the ulama represents, then, the final path for the Islamicization of the country, and it is an a priori assumption in this literature. In other words, the institutions in the country must be changed to correspond to this consensus. The opposite case has not received the attention it deserves, especially in discussions of economic issues. My objective is to try to fill this gap.

After the establishment of Pakistan, the politicians adopted a 'constitutional' approach to the demand for establishing an Islamic state, hoping to diffuse the pressure from the ulama. They did not seem inclined to accept the views of the ulama, but they made solemn declarations that they envisaged a country in which Muslims would be free to build their lives in accordance with Islam. Perhaps they had considerable confidence in their ability to exercise an ambidextrous strategy and each of them hoped that this strategy would see him through the term of his office. Or, perhaps they expected that somehow some kind of Islamic modernism would evolve in the long run and resolve this conflict for them. They were not men of vision and they had no courage of their conviction. In order to develop and foster modernist thought, it was necessary to establish a framework for free and open discussion, accepting and tolerating dissent. It was imperative that teaching and research at universities be diligently promoted. No serious effort was made in this direction. When General Ziaul Haq came to power, he found ample opportunity to turn the perfervid rhetoric about Islamicization to his advantage.

The emergence of Islamic economics during the seventies and eighties was based on the position of the traditionalist ulama concerning economic issues such as interest-free banking, the religious tax of *zakat*, and the laws of inheritance, as established and interpreted by the classical jurists. The objective was to provide a framework for the legitimate activities of the pious Muslim entrepreneurs working towards the creation of what was called the Islamic welfare economy in the country. Through this new literature, albeit moulded in juristic vocabulary, it became possible to hinder the cause of modernism in the country. What has in fact emerged is a phenomenon familiar in Muslim history, that of economic factors responding to the challenge of the Islamic reforms by means of subterfuges to get around them. This question has international implications as well. The fact that the nature of capital has changed drastically over the last fifty years, and the fact that capital has become almost completely dedomiciled, there are limits to experimenting with Islamic reforms such as interest-free banking in the context of the global economy. This issue, however, requires a separate study.

The book presents a critical discussion of the Islamic economic system which was introduced during the regime of General Ziaul Haq. I take the position, however, that the Islamicization of General Ziaul Haq was a logical consequence following the position established by the Objectives Resolution, as well as the principles of Islamic policy which were enunciated in the 1973 Constitution. Also, Zulfikar Ali Bhutto during his tenure as Prime Minister introduced some Islamic reforms which paved the way smoothly for the General. This is explained in Chapter I. In Chapters II to IV, I examine critically the subject matter of Islamic economics, emphasizing its neoclassical roots; I suggest that when Islamic banking is practised in the framework of a modern interest-based economy, it becomes a special form of banking, broadening and diversifying the financial structure of the country; and I also emphasize that the Islamic modes of financing are incompatible with modern economic realities, if they are defined in their 'pure' form with a clearly identifiable risk taken by an individual. In Chapter V, attention is drawn to the androcentric bias of the laws of inheritance. The question of the Islamic economic system is discussed in Chapter VI, in the context of the historical development of the Islamic civilization. Chapter VII deals with the question of women in Islam as an example of the battle of ideas, in the context of the historical development of the currently-held views of the traditionalists about women. In Chapter VIII, I sum up my argument on the scope for Islamic modernism, and I suggest that the issue of the long-term economic goals for the country cannot be resolved until the larger question concerning the nature of the state is settled. In my concluding remarks I discuss the divergence between words and deeds that has developed as a persistent phenomenon in the Islamic Republic of Pakistan. It stems from the assumption that responsibility of the state is to implement Islam as a complete code of life. But it creates a paradox. The individual is expected to submit to the Will of God voluntarily in order to be pious. The Will of God, however, is expressed not through exaltation of personal faith in action, but only through the state regulating his life.

The fiftieth anniversary of Pakistan took place under Nawaz Sharif as the prime minister of the country. The government of Benazir Bhutto was dissolved in November 1996, leading to new elections and return of Mr Sharif as the new national leader. Ms Bhutto was under the cloud of accusations of corruption and nepotism. During her regime, no major piece of legislation was introduced or passed by the National Assembly, with the notable exception of the Prohibition of Whipping Act. It may be said that most of her attention was devoted towards maintaining legitimacy of her government, towards the difficulties faced by the country in structural adjustment, and to debt and deficit. One might be inclined to conclude, then, that the question of Islamic reforms has been receding into the background.

This would be a serious misjudgement of the situation. The legacy of Islamicization of General Ziaul Haq remains intact. The question of *riba* is still unsettled, pending a hearing by the Supreme Court since 1992. Also, when Mr Nawaz Sharif was Prime Minister during 1990–92, the Sharia Act was passed by the National Assembly under his leadership. The Act has serious implications as it seems to contradict some of the provisions of the constitution of the country. Which direction Mr Nawaz Sharif would follow in his second incarnation remains an open question.

CHAPTER 1

The State and the Economy[1]

The institutions which a country develops to achieve its social and economic objectives impinge significantly on the pattern of its economic growth. In the case of Pakistan, the relation between the state and the society is being defined in the framework of Islam and the task seems to have become an elusive goal. No real progress has been made in this direction in spite of repetitive declarations about the Islamic character of the country. In fact, there is no consensus, even among the ulama, about what constitutes an Islamic community.

Pakistan has been in search of its identity since its establishment in August 1947. This struggle has been compounded by the fact that the origins of the idea of Pakistan diverge completely from the political forces which have been defining and redefining the country for the last five decades. Muslim nationalism from the time of Sir Syed Ahmad Khan to Muhammad Ali Jinnah was fostered by secular-minded intellectuals and leaders, seeking protection of the Indian Muslim culture from the Hindu-dominated majority (Aziz 1987c: 726ff.). The poet-philosopher Sir Muhammad Iqbal, for example, is revered as one of the founders of Pakistan. In fact, he proposed the formation of a new entity consisting of the Muslim majority in the north-western region of a united India (Aziz 1987a: 313ff.). During the period of the Pakistan movement in the 1940s, M.A. Jinnah was seeking a solution whereby the Muslim majority provinces as a 'state' (or 'states') would share responsibility of government in a new central Indian consitutional arrangement (Jalal 1985). For him the

Muslims would be free under this arrangement to determine their lives in a democratic process, based on the principles of Islam.

The new Muslim nation was born in 1947, and it was gradually to become an 'Islamic' state under the impact of the domestic political forces. The Islamic idealogy was to play a role, but it was not dominant or virtually autonomous of the area of social existence around it. It was really contingent on the specific circumstances relating to social support and conjunctures which had emerged in the country.[2] Jinnah, as the founder of the new nation, did not have the opportunity to delineate in categorical terms his own conception about Pakistan. During the short period of about a year that he survived in 1947–8, he was faced with the horrendous refugee problems, apart from the questions of financial and administrative stability of the country. And he was at the same time trying to cope with his fatal illness. The often-quoted passage from his address to the new Constituent Assembly, delivered on 11 August 1947, seems to suggest that Pakistan was to be a secular democratic state, in which all citizens would have equal rights irrespective of caste, creed or religion (Munir n.d., 29ff.). However, a few months later, in 1948, he told the members of the Sind Bar Associastion to prepare themselves to make Pakistan a truly great Islamic state (Jalal 1990: 279). Then, later that year, he told his audience at the convocation of Dhaka University that Urdu would be the official language of the country, with Bengali as one of the regional languages (Jahan 1972). He knew that this message would not go down well with his Bengali audience. He had less than working proficiency in the language, but had obviously come to the conclusion that Urdu would serve as a stronger binding force for the two wings of the country, having its roots in Persian and Arabic languages and with deeper links with the Islamic culture. How far he would have been willing to compromise his secular views had he lived long enough to preside over the new constitution remains an open question.

The circumstances in which the August 1947 speech was delivered had drastically changed, as a result of the unprecedented refugee problems created by the partition of the Punjab. In the newly created East Pakistan out of the old province of Bengal, the numerical strength of Hindus had also declined. This fact was not lost on the advocates of the idea of the Islamic state for Pakistan, such as Abul A'la Maudoodi, the then head of the Jama'at-e-Islami (Munir: 33ff.). He had opposed Jinnah's plan for the partition of British India. Nevertheless he opted in favour of Pakistan rather than remaining an Indian national. He was aware that the propelling force behind the Pakistan movement was a modernist and Western-educated elite. The common people, however, perceived of the new state in terms of the ideology of Islam. The population upheaval caused by the partition of India left West Pakistan as an overwhelmingly Muslim region, though Hindus still formed a reasonable minority in East Pakistan. Also, the Muslims of independent India soon realized that they were no longer protected by Jinnah's two-nation theory; they had become a minority in the new India.

It must be emphasized, nevertheless, that Jinnah's commitment to the idea of Pakistan was to create a Muslim-majority state, not an Islamic state. That is what the well-known 1940 Resolution envisaged, and his efforts to avoid the partition of Punjab during the last few months of the Pakistan movement would seem to fit in well with his objective. He knew that Islam had a strong appeal for Muslim masses and he had made use of it during his campaign. In this respect his role in 1947–8 was consistent with his past performance. The only question is whether he would have been able to contain the forces which had been unleashed in the context of the changed circumstances of what he called a truncated and moth-eaten Pakistan. This question must await a comprehensive assessment of Jinnah's place in the history of Pakistan.

The Objectives Resolution

The structure of the new country began with the existential reality of a secular organization of its government, but religion started to be invoked to counter the rising tide of provincialism and ethnic tensions (Jalal 1990: Chap. 6). After Jinnah's death, Liaquat Ali Khan became the undisputed leader of the country, consolidating his power as the Prime Minister. He encountered pressure from religious groups about the Islamic character of the state. The ulama such as Maulana Shabbir Ahmed Usmani who had played an important part in the Pakistan movement in Bengal, or Pir of Manki Sharif who had been quite influential in the referendum in the North-West Frontier Province, brought to bear considerable influence from within the Muslim League in this regard. Abul A'la Maudoodi saw his opportunity to play a role and put forward his 'four demands' for making Pakistan an Islamic state (Binder 1963). In addition, there were other problems relating to the federal structure comprising East and West Pakistan. A solemn declaration in the form of the Objectives Resolution passed by the Constituent Assembly in 1949 was considered to be a step in the right direction to control the situation.

The Objectives Resolution, in fact, was to provide constitutional legitimacy to the phenomenon—the myth of the Islamic state[3]—that was to emerge in the form of a dichotomy between the secular state and Islamic Law and it has continued with all its attendant problems to haunt the politics of the country since 1947. The Resolution was a masterpiece of vague platitudes, and it represented a complete departure from Jinnah's speech of August 1947. It declared that sovereignty over the entire universe belonged to God, and that it had been delegated to the State of Pakistan through its people, to enable the Muslims to order their lives in accordance with Islam, and to make adequate provisions for minorities to profess and practice their religion and culture (Mahmood 1975). The first Draft Constitution submitted in 1950 contained a brief statement promising that the Objectives Resolution would guide the activities of the government. The second Draft Constitution submitted in 1952, after the death of Liaquat Ali Khan, extended the promise by incoporating in it the so-called 'repugnancy clause' in order to make sure that no laws were in contravention of the Qur'an and the Sunna. The head of the state was to constitute an advisory board for this purpose. In 1954, however, the Supreme Court was given the specific powers to determine whether any laws were repugnant to Islam. In 1956 when the new Constituent Assembly was established, the constitution provided for a new organization for Islamic research and instruction, replacing the supreme court by a commission appointed by the president and giving it the powers to make suitable recommendations regarding the matter.

The Constitution of 1956 provided for a federal system of government based on two wings of Pakistan, with East Pakistan as one unit and with the three provinces of West Pakistan combined constituting the other unit. It incorporated a new clause in the preamble (the Objectives Resolution) referring to the declaration by the 'Founder of Pakistan' that 'Pakistan would be a democratic State based on Islamic principles of social justice...' (Mahmood 1975: 215). The political instability that had plagued the country from 1948 became much worse with total deterioration in the quality of leadership during this period. There were four prime ministers in a short span of less than two years. The farce of the so-called democracy was brought to an end by the declaration of martial law and emergence of General Ayub Khan in 1958 as the Chief Martial Law Administrator and then later as president.

With Ayub Khan, a new experiment in controlled democracy started in the country. Under the 1962 Constitution of the Second Republic, the Objectives Resolution was amended so that in the first clause

concerning sovereignty of God and the authority exercised
by the people of Pakistan the phrase 'within the limits
prescribed by Him' was deleted. The country was to
become the Republic of Pakistan, and the prefix 'Islamic'
was removed; it had been inserted first in the report of the
Basic Principles Committee in 1954 and had become part
of the 1956 Constitution. There was to be an Advisory
Council of Islamic Ideology, to be appointed by the
president, and its main function was to make
recommendations as to means of enabling Muslims to order
their lives in accordance with Islam, but without the shadow
of the 'repugnancy clause'. Also, there was to be an Islamic
Research Institute and its purpose was to assist in the
reconstruction of Muslim society on a truly Islamic basis.
(Mahmood: 503ff.)

The new constitution seemed to promise the beginning of
a new era, to build a modern Muslim society and to
reconstruct the Islamic thought accordingly. This was an
objective upon which all Muslims who were weary of the
politicians playing up to the mullahs, could have complete
agreement, irrespective of the various shades of opinions
among them concerning the role of Islam in the country. It
seems that their optimism was short-lived. The First
Amendment issued in January 1964, reinstated the
'repugnancy' clause and added that the application of this
principle to the personal law of any Muslim sect shall be the
Qur'an and *Sunna* as interpreted by that sect. It further stated
that the Advisory Council of Islamic Ideology would examine
all laws immediately in order to bring them into conformity
with Islam. This represented a retreat to the status quo
ante, and it was obviously in response to the pressures
from the traditional ulama, especially the Jama'at-e-Islami.
In 1963, Professor Fazlur Rahman, the then Director of
the Islamic Research Institute wrote an essay on interest
and usury, in which he argued that the Qur'anic prohibition
against *riba* was not applicable to the modern banking
system. Abul A'la Maudoodi and other ulama found this

to be unacceptable, and they led an unedifying campaign against him and consequently he had to resign. This further compromised the position of Ayub Khan as President of Pakistan (Feldman 1967: 94). He resigned in 1969 and the political fortunes of the republic fluctuated until Zulfikar Ali Bhutto came to power when West Pakistan became Pakistan, with East Pakistan emerging as an independent Bangladesh.

The main focus in the remaining Pakistan was once again on the constitution for the new country. In April 1973, the National Assembly approved a new draft of the Constitution of the Islamic Republic of Pakistan. It was the result of intense negotiations among various groups in the National Assembly, and it reflected 'some heavy compromises with the religious right...' (Rahman 1973: 190) The preamble of the Constitution was amended and in the second paragraph '...the Founder of Pakistan...' was deleted and the declaration simply expressed the will of the people to establish an order. This paved the way to declaration that 'Islam shall be the state religion of Pakistan' (Mahmood 1975). The Advisory Council of Islamic Ideology became the Council of Islamic Ideology (CII), and it was to consist of eight to fifteen members with adequate representation from judges and scholars of Islam, and was also to have a female representative. The CII. was required to submit its findings within seven years of its appointment and make recommendations with a view to bringing all existing laws in conformity with the injunctions of Islam.

The country was to become a parliamentary democracy, replacing the presidential system of the 1962 Constitution as enacted by General Ayub Khan. Pakistan embarked upon a new era with Z.A. Bhutto as the prime minister. There were many political developments in this period, but the Islamic provisions of the Constitution were really not put to test, except that the weekly holiday was changed from Sunday to Friday and sale of liquor to Muslims was banned. Further playing up to the ulama, Bhutto had the National Assembly declare members of the Qadiani and Ahmedi sects non-Muslims in 1974. The first general elections in the country were held in March 1977, and these elections turned out to be a major contributing factor in the downfall of Bhutto.

General Ziaul Haq took over as the chief martial law administrator, and gradually began his Islamicization policy as a self-proclaimed defender of Islam. From the time of the Objectives Resolution as passed by the Constituent Assembly in 1949 to the 1973 Constitution, the religious declarations had been largely used as exhortations for the Muslims to follow the right path. These declarations were received by the ulama as a very modest step in the right direction. For the modernist secular politicians, however, the vagueness and lack of definition of these pronouncements were reassuring, and they felt that these pronouncements would cause no real change in their usual political pursuits. The exploitation of Islam for political purposes from Liaquat Ali Khan to Zulfikar Ali Bhutto provided an opportunity to Ziaul Haq to use religion for his legitimacy with some well-designed changes in the 1973 Constitution, while some parts of it were held in abeyance 'on account of state necessity.' He introduced the concept of *majlis-e-shoora* as his advisory council, amended the document in order to provide for the *zakat* and *ushr* schemes, and added a provision for the establishment of federal shariat courts, giving them powers to decide if any laws were repugnant to Islam. As for the Council of Islamic Ideology, he reconstituted its membership to reflect a clear fundamentalist bias, and introduced compulsory *zakat* fund and 'interest-free' banking on the recommendations of the Council. By the end of 1985 martial law was withdrawn and the Constitution was amended to give additional powers to Ziaul Haq as President, and to incorporate in it the martial law regulations, decisions and orders. The Objectives Resolution which had served as the preamble of the Consitution ever since 1956 was made its substantive part at the same time (Lahore Law Times, n.d.). Also, the Resolution now assured minorities that adequate provisions shall be made to profess their religions, not 'freely' to profess their religions as was stated in the original (1973) Resolution. The politicization of Islam had come full circle during the regime of Ziaul Haq.

The next important development in the political manoeuvring of the Islamic ideology took place in 1991 under the leadership of Nawaz Sharif as Prime Minister and head of a coalition called the Islami Jamhoori Ittehad (the Islamic Democratic Alliance) consisting of the secular Muslim League and the religious parties. This was done in the form of the Sharia Act passed by the National Assembly in May 1991. The preamble to the Act made it 'obligatory for Muslims to follow the injunctions of Islam' whereas the Objectives Resolution had only declared that the 'Muslims shall be enabled to order their lives' in accordance with the teachings of Islam. The explanatory paragraph under sections 1 and 2 calls for 'recognized principles' to aid interpretation of the *sharia* and towards this goal to take into consideration the 'expositions and opinions of recognised jurists of Islam' belonging to the prevalent schools of jusrisprudence. It is not clear whether the Act requires measures for an active role of the ulama, in addition to those provided for the Council of Islamic Ideology. Section 3 of the Act makes *sharia* the supreme law of Pakistan, and by implication, raises questions about the status of the constitution itself. The Act calls for the establishment of commissions to make recommendations for Islamicization of the educational system and the economy of the country (Mehdi 1994: Appendix III).

The Sharia Act is vague and repetitive and gives the appearance of a political manifesto. Nevertheless, it leaves plenty of room for the clerics to manoeuvre if and when they find another Ziaul Haq to lead them to their cherished goal. Also, by focusing on the *sharia*, it underlines the basic problem facing Pakistan. How would *sharia* be defined with reference to the Qur'an and *Sunna*, when there are substantial differences among Muslims concerning the interpretation of the Qur'anic text and serious differences about the traditions of the Holy Prophet. The country is facing sharp divisions among the religious sects and is divided more than ever on ethnic lines. The gap between the dream of an Islamic state and the reality of the actual state of affairs is wider than ever in the country.

The State and National Goals

The Objectives Resolution was an attempt to reconcile the place of Islam in establishing a territorial state with Muslim majority in the country. It may be said, however, that the establishment of Pakistan had rendered irrelevant the conflict between ideological and territorial nationalism from the point of view of Islam. During the Pakistan movement, the ulama, especially of the Deoband School, disagreed with the supporters of Pakistan concerning what constituted a nation in Islam. The exchange between Maulana Hussain Ahmed Madani and Sir Muhammad Iqbal in 1937 underlined the controversy. Iqbal in a poem had condemned Maulana's attitude and the Maulana had in response claimed that Islam accepted the existence of nations comprising Muslims as well as non-Muslims in a country (Zakaria 1989: 5ff).

For Iqbal there was no dichotomy between religion and state in the sense that politics must have an ethical foundation. Abul A'la Maudoodi also believed that in Islam, religion and politics could not be separated. However, he took a clearly fundamentalist position on the issue, arguing for the establishment of the order on lines as exemplified by the period of the Prophet and the four 'rightly guided' caliphs of Islam. In his post-1947 position, the universalism of Islam underwent a rapid modification.

Sovereignty for him still belonged to God but it was to be defined in terms of the territorial nationalism of Pakistan, in order to make the country a truly Islamic state. Referring to the Qur'anic verses where words such as *hukm* (authority) and *amr* (order) were used, he argued that government could only be of divine origin. He invoked verse 12:40 ('authority belongs to God only'), for example, in support of his view. The context of the verse, however, makes it clear that it is polytheism that is being condemnded, not the conduct of public affairs (Boularés 1990: 77ff).

The declaration confirming sovereignty of God in the Objectives Resolution was a tacit acceptance of the claim that law is a fixed code and can only be interpreted by the ulama. It embarked the country on to a slippery road in search of its identity. Maudoodi was an ideological essentialist. However, Pakistan was the product of interaction of Indian politics and the British resolve to withdraw from the subcontinent. Both new countries were to become members of the Commonwealth and were to be integrated into the wider global economic system. The title of Islamic Republic established the duality as the term 'republic' underlined its links with the evolution of the European system of government. This phenomenon was to generate political tensions as it has throughout the history of the country. In this framework, a bid for power would lead to the exclusive control of the state, as it did with General Ziaul Haq, with the purported objective of rejecting alien institutions in favour of a truly Islamic set-up. General Ziaul Haq followed his Islamicization policies with great fervour, and with the support of the ulama, using his edicts and orders as the chief martial law administrator. Nevertheless, the goal of creating an Islamic state eluded him, and at best his regime could be called a 'pious sultan' administration in which the religious elements supported his rule in exchange for drafting laws in accordance with the Islamic objectives as interpreted by them. His role in the Afghanistan war created a new culture in which guns and drugs started to permeate the fabric of the Pakistan society, and this phenomenon is still haunting the country. Above all, his Islamicization has created deep divisions between modernists and traditionalists, caused fears among the members of the small non-Muslim minorities, and promoted schism among the various religious sects in the country.

Zulfikar Ali Bhutto established Islam as the state religion in the country. General Ziaul Haq took it a few steps further in order to Islamicize the country. In both cases, there was a clear recognition that the reality of a sovereign state with its territorial boundaries was to be the reference point for reform. In the classification of states as offered by Ibn Khaldun, Pakistan is a *mulk* (country, state) in which government authority is based on a mixture of power, politics and the sharia. (Rosenthal 1965: 17ff). With all the force of the Objectives Resolution and the Sharia Act, the goal of an Islamic state is still unrealized.

Pakistan then is a sovereign Muslim state. Is it also a nation? During the period of the Pakistan movement in the 1940s, M.A. Jinnah always emphasized that Indian Muslims were a separate nation. After the establishment of Pakistan, that claim lost its legitimacy as Muslims found themselves divided between two countries. In Pakistan Islam was the common factor among the majority of its people, with five distinct linguistic groups and a multiplicity of castes and sub-castes. It was assumed that the people of Pakistan were united under the banner of their religion. The phenomenon of Islamic solidarity, however, was not strong enough to keep East Pakistan as part of the country, and it emerged as an independent Bangladesh after the bloody battle fought in 1971. It may be argued that the absence of geographical contiguity between the two wings of the country weakened its unity and led ultimately to the creation of two independent states. Also, it may be pointed out that the economies of the two wings were very dissimilar, and the standard of living in East Pakistan was considerably lower than in West Pakistan. During the first decades after the establishment of Pakistan, the two regions did not indicate any semblance of integration, or a common ground (Jahan 1972: 35ff). From the point of view of the Bengalis it was a case of internal colonialism. Perhaps it became a circle within a circle, because during the Pakistan movement the uneven regional economic development was a contributing factor in the grievances of the Muslims in the north-east and north-west India.

Michael Hechtor's model of internal colonialism, therefore, would have some relevance to explain the above phenomenon (Hechtor 1975). His model as he originally applied to Britain was perhaps open to criticism. He had claimed a cultural division of labour with the English as colonizers and the Scots, Welsh and Irish as the colonized. The rise of ethnic nationalism weakened his thesis, though he revised it and used the concept of 'segmental cultural division of labour' to explain the situation, emphasizing the vertical rather than hierarchical stratification in the society (Hechter 1985). The structure of internal colonialism perhaps may not be as significant as other elements making up a nationalist organization; his model nevertheless remains a compelling one in the context of multi-ethnic and multi-religious societies in South Asia and other similar regions.

Pakistan shrunken in size after the secession of Bangladesh, comprising only the four provinces of Balochistan, Frontier, Punjab, and Sindh along with the princely states such as Kalat and Bahawalpur merged with the new country, cannot really claim to be a homogeneous nation. With Bangladesh gone, it is overwhelmingly a Muslim country. Religion obviously unites people, but it also creates divisiveness among them. The majority of Pakistani Muslims profess Sunni Islam, but it is still a very heterodox place, with hundreds of idiosyncratic, often ethnically based sufi brotherhood, as well as a significant minority claiming Shi'ism. The division is further compounded by the fact that each of them shares the idea that it is the best and purest form of faith (Pastner 1987: 31).

Ethnic rectitude is a concomitant of this climate. There is a feeling of alienation among the non-Punjabis as the Punjabi dominate the civil and military services in the country. The policy to have Urdu as the official language, on one hand, seems to have given no special sense of security to the Urdu-speaking migrants from India. On the other, it has encouraged ethnic reassertion among the Balochis, Sindhis, and Pakhtoons. Also the sense of brotherhood as claimed by the proponents of *Nizam-e-Islam* is obviously not sufficiently strong to promote integration of refugees as illustrated by the conflict between the muhajir and Sindhis.

How to create a nation, then, in which pluralistic realities are accomodated, and there is unity in spite of diversity promoting territorial integrity of the state. The question is considered irrelevant from the point of view of traditionalist Islam, as the objective of Islamicization is to create the *homo-Islamicus* in the true image of the pristine period of the Prophet and the four pious caliphs. This is where the rhetoric of the Islamic state and the reality of the Muslim state diverge and the rhetoric continues to obfuscate the reality, while the situation clamours for practical solutions.

The relation between the nation and the state is quite complex. People may live in a strong state as was the case with the Hamberg Empire or the Ottoman Empire, and may still not be considered a nation. In fact the American started the modern trend of nation states because the people who had settled in the new world wanted to determine their own affairs in spite of linguistic or religious affinities with their native European regions. In Europe, Germans claimed to be a nation based on language. France and Britain each established a state, gradually creating sovereignty and strengthening and making it durable by centralizing kings who were able to defeat particularistic tendencies in the territories controlled by them (Kedourie 1960: 77). There is no plain method whereby nations may be isolated from one another. 'The world is indeed diverse, much too diverse, for the classification of nationalist anthropology. Race, languages, religions, political traditions, and loyalties are so inextricably intermixed that there can be no clear convincing reason why people who speak the same language, but whose history and circumstances otherwise widely diverge, should form one state, or why people who speak two different languages and whose circumstances have thrown them together should not form one state' (Kedourie 1960: 79).

When we talk of national economic strategy, what characteristics are required which may be commonly shared by the citizens of the state? For Gellner, nationalism is a response to uneven economic development. He believes that it has escaped the grasp of nineteenth century liberalism and Marxism as both were skeptical about the phenomenon (Gellner 1983). There is a superficial similarity here with Hechter's theory, but Gellner suggests that a particular form of polity and culture are required for industrialization and these forms combine in the nation-state. Educational system plays a crucial role in this process as workers, managers, and bureaucrats must be trained who would use a common language, which in turn would provide for mobility and division of labour.

Benedict Anderson, unlike Gellner, emphasizes ideology of nationalism as a cultural artefact (Anderson 1983). His main point is to explain why people in certain circumstances come to 'imagine' themselves as part of a nation. He cites Gellner approvingly but says that the emotional power of nationalism invents nations where they do not exist. Taking a historical approach, he looks at the cultural systems of religious communities. For example, in the early Islamic *umma* the binding force was the sacred text which they all shared in the classical Arabic. However, like the Christian community, the Islamic community was gradually fragmented, pluralized and territorialized (Anderson 1983: 12ff). Similarly, the dynastic rules underwent radical change, as Europe advanced into the modern age, and factors such as print capitalism served as the main instruments by which people would make 'pilgrimages' in their social and economic lives, thus defining the boundaries of their nation.

Looking at the question in the context of Pakistan, the nation was 'invented' to promote social and economic development without the fear of Hindu domination. The pilgrimage then was supposed to have been the mental process involved in establishing the relationship among the people, based on the above assumption. The objective was to create a civil society with a truly representative government which would exercise an effective control over the economy. This objective has not materialized. The events as they have gradually unfolded in the last five decades of Pakistan's existence cannot really be examined from the point of the World Bank criteria of good governance (World Bank, 1992). It is not a question concerning the relevance of these criteria. Their main limitation is that they are based on a narrow technocratic approach and their focus is the Bank's programme of structural adjustment, and its neo-liberal agenda to promote market economy. The soft state versus strong state concept of Gunnar Myrdal (Myrdal 1968: Chap.3 and Appendix 9), underlines the broader issue relating to administrative values and attitudes which may help or hinder a country's progress. Its basic assumption, however, is dirigiste.

Both the neo-liberal and the dirigiste approaches clearly indicate that sustained economic development in a developing country is the product of the patterns of politics which tend to concentrate in the state both the will and the competence to establish a developmental momentum (Leftwich 1994: 373). In this respect, Marx's concept of an autonomous state may have some relevance for our perspective. He suggested that such a state arose as a result of balance of class forces under Louis Bonaparte, pursuing its interests by harnessing those of others to its purpose (Elster 1985: 426). The Bonapartist state, however, arose in a situation very different from what may be happening in Pakistan. There was the militant working class, for example, which needed to be controlled, and the state rested on the social support of the conservative peasantry in the country (Halliday 1979: 52). Nevertheless, it is important to understand and identify the forces which have helped the state machine, as against the civil society, to gradually consolidate its position as an autonomous entity in Pakistan. Also, it is important to note how Islamic ideology has been used as a cloak for vested interests, so that some groups could derive strength from it by reaffirming their faith in Islam and others would try to push action programme under its name. During the 1950s, the state became the converging point for the feudal, bureaucratic and bourgeois interests (Alavi 1983: 62–4). The role of the military emerged slowly as the politicians needed its support for their legitimacy and became an important element in the country.

The first Constituent Assembly of Pakistan came into being through an indirect elective process and as a result of regional division of seats corresponding to the partition of the subcontinent. It also inherited its legislative powers from the Indian Independence Act, 1947. With the passage of time, as the constitutional debates dragged on, the Constituent Assembly losts its prestige. The second Constituent Assembly was formed in 1955, again through an indirect elective process, and while it was deliberating on the matters put before it, the governor-generals, the presidents, and the prime ministers were rapidly shifting positions like in the game of the musical chairs. Then, as mentioned above, General Ayub Khan led the country from 1958 to 1969 under his controlled democracy. With Zulfikar Ali Bhutto (from 1971 to 1977), a permanent constitution was at last promulgated. The contradictions of the constitution became obvious under General Ziaul Haq, and the country since Ziaul Haq has seen the experiments of the Muslim League and the People's Party governments alternatively, depending upon the political situation. The former claims its commitment to Ziaul Haq's Islamicization, and the latter seems to treat these Islamic reforms with a degree of indifference. General elections have been held, on party basis, in 1988, 1990, 1993 and 1997. Does this auger well for democracy in Pakistan?

Democracy and Islam

The relationship between state and society is quite complex. It is determined by historial factors, both internal and external, as well as the level of economic development of the country. The so-called East Asian miracle of economic growth gave rise to a whole new body of literature during the sixties and the seventies eulogizing the virtues of authoritative and interventionist regimes devoted to the promotion of industrialization and foreign trade.[4] It seems, however, that this phenomenon is more complex than the question of government-business relations. There is nevertheless a paradox here in the story of East Asian success, and the recent financial crisis facing the region clearly underlines this fact. Behind the facade of free enterprise, the East Asian regimes, in most cases, were promoting crony capitalism, and their economies were far from meeting the criteria of the market system.

The link between the form of a government and response of the business to it is not well-established. It is partly because the state in Pakistan, in spite of shifting political elite, has looked after the interests of the entrepreneurial class, and partly owing to the fact that the success of this class has depended largely on the cycles of national and international economic environment. Pakistan is a parliamentary democracy, according to the 1973

Constitution, with Islam as the state religion, and with equality for all citizens before the law irrespective of race, religion, or gender. Not all political groups, however, are united on these basic assumptions of the Constitution. The Islamic state, as defined by Maudoodi, will be a theo-democracy. It will be a democracy because the head of the state will be appointed through a procedure which will ensure that he enjoys confidence of the people. It will be a theocracy because only the head of the state, after consultation with the pious Muslims, and being more equal than the rest of them, will interpret the Islamic code in the framework of sovereignty of God. In Maudoodi's Islamic society, the non-Muslims will be treated as a protected minority (Ahmed, Zafaryab, 1985; Ahmed, Ishtiaq, 1987).

Maudoodi's views are not shared by other Islamic scholars. Professor Fazlur Rahman, for example, believes that an Islamic state will be completely democratic, though the parliamentary system would be unsuitable for it, in view of the fact that a strong executive head is envisaged by the Qur'an. Also, there would be no multi-party system as practised in modern democracies because Islam is averse to opposition for the sake of opposition. For him, 'Sovereinty of God' as used by Maudoodi is an absurd concept. The Muslim legislature would be a supreme body except for limitations imposed by the Qur'an (Rahman 1976). Fazlur Rahman does not directly discuss the status of non-Muslims but it can safely be assumed that, in his view, they would not play a role in the legislative process for establishing Islamic laws in the country.

The poet-philospher Iqbal believes that the Law of Islam is capable of evolution and that it would be necessary to transfer the powers of reinterpretation of the Law from individual representatives of schools of jurisprudence to a Muslim legislative assembly. This assembly would be guided but not supervised by the ulama (Iqbal 1951: Chap. 6). Khalifa Abdul Hakim is of the view that a truly Muslim state would possess all the good qualities of a secular state without being secular in the modern sense. The president of the country could be appointed through an election, or he might be chosen from a panel of names already approved by the Muslims. He emphasizes that Islamic law is fixed as well as flexible and that there is plenty of scope for a legislative body in an Islamic state (Hakim 1953)

The assumptions of the 1973 Constitution require a stable civil society, and Pakistan has been evolving in several directions all, albeit slowly, leading towards that goal. There is a growing industrial elite and an expanding middle class in urban centres of the country. Education opportunities have improved at least for those who can afford them, and there is some concern about the facilities lagging for women and the poor in this regard. There is a degree of prosperity accompanied by the use of modern durable goods. Parallel to these indices, however, there are some disturbing signs which cast a shadow of doubt on the future prospects. In so far as the civil is the converse of the military, it has special relevance as the military became the source and instrument of power in the country, as a legacy of Ziaul Haq. Now that the Article 58 (2b) has been deleted from the Constitution, taking away powers of the president arbitrarily to dismiss the elected government, the old scenario which gave the military the proxy role seems to have disappeared, though it still commands a major item of expenditure in the national budget. The new political pattern, however, in this regard is not easy to predict. The feudal class and the landed aristocracy continue to dominate the political scene and tend to hamper the modernization of the economy. Also, civility is on the decline as there is lack of tolerance among various sects and the life and liberty of non-Muslims do not always seem to be well protected. In theory, the Islamic state is supposed to promote peace and harmony among people. But, the blasphemy laws enacted through various ordinances by General Ziaul Haq during 1980–86, and the ruling of the Federal Shariat Court in 1990 imposing death penalty for this crime, and the consequences following this ruling, tend to demonstrate how an atmosphere of inquisition could be created in the name of religion, so that the poison of hatred would encourage forces degenerating the social order.

There are, in addition, perceived or real concerns about high level of corruption, inaccountability, police brutality, administrative inefficiency, as well as the role of judiciary, and there are real pressures of ever-increasing cost of living and of growing shortages of basic needs. If these tendencies can be stemmed, democracy may have a chance in the country. And the modernists who follow Iqbal and Khalifa Abdul Hakim, by applying the broad principles enunciated by them, and in the spirit of renewed pragmatism, may recognize the importance of pluralism in a modern society built on the Islamic values. It must be emphasized, however, that when people lose hope in their leaders, and the system these leaders represent, then they may welcome the proponents of theo-democracy as a liberating force.

The fabric of democracy in Pakistan is very fragile. It is partly owing to the social realities facing the country and it may partly be attributed to the penumbra of the Objective Resolution and the 'repugnancy' clause as these two sections of the Constitution will continue to give the ulama the tools to extert their pressures on democracy, limiting its scope in the name of Islam. Also, the fact that the Qur'an and *Sunna* may be applied to the personal laws affecting any members of a sect in accordance with the interpretation of that sect will tend to interfere in any effort for a comprehensive reconstruction of religious thought in the country. The original intention of this constitutional provision might have been to promote unity, but in fact it would cause disharmony and sectarian conflict. The real challenge is to search for a common ground among the various interpretations of the Muslim personal law, and there is no sign that the importance of this challenge is being recognized among the politicians and the educated elite of the country. It seems that in a society where the feudal class enjoys a place far out of proportion to its size, the militant ulama do not seem to present a threat to the status quo in Pakistan.

The question of democracy in Pakistan cannot be easily explained with the help of facile generalizations concerning state and society in Islam. The Orientalists and the neo-Orientalists, for example, seem to believe in the cliché concerning the inseparability of Church and State in an Islamic society. The former emphasize that the Muslim state would necessarily be authoritarian as it would suffer from a lack of assertive social groups. For the latter, the authoritarianism is the consequence of 'pushy, anarchic solitudes' (Sadowsky, 1993).[5] Whatever the validity of these two contradictory positions, ahistorical view about the mysterious 'essence' of Islam is completely irrelevant in the case of Pakistan.

NOTES

1. This chapter incorporates material from my article entitled 'Pakistan, Islam and Economics', published in the *Journal of Contemporary Asia*, Vol. 17, No. 2, 1987.

2. Fred Halliday and Hamza Alavi (1988) emphasize this point in their Introduction to the book as a lesson of history of the Muslim states in recent years.

3. P.J. Vatikiotis (1987) explains the phenomenon and refers to it as a myth of the Islamic state, p. 9. *See also,* Nazih Ayubi (1991) for a discussion of the role of utopia in the theory of the Islamic state.

4. S.P. Hungtington (1968), *Political Order in a Changing Society* is a notable contribution on the subject. *See also,* C. Johnson (1987), 'Political Institutions and Economic Progress: The Government-Business Relations in Japan, South Korea and Taiwan', in F.C. Deyo (1987). For a critical assessment of this hypothesis *see,* T. Killick (1989).

5. Yahya Sadowski (1993) presents a good review on this issue and suggests that serious scholars should turn to the matter-of-fact itemization of the forces that promote or retard the democratic process in the Muslim countries.

CHAPTER 2

Economics and Islamic Economics

The literature on Islamic economics is purported to present a third alternative to the other two main economic systems, capitalism and socialism. The emphasis in this literature, however, is mainly on monetary and fiscal analysis of an economy based on *zakat* on wealth and profit-and-loss sharing rate of return on capital. The a priori assumptions of this analysis are those of the neoclassical theory. There is some discussion on the subject matter of Islamic economics as a separate discipline, but it seems to be an extension of the neoclassical logic with a view to what are claimed to be the Islamic improvements in the mainstream economics.

The development of a separate discipline of Islamic economics has probably reached a plateau, beginning with the decade of the nineties. One of the foremost Islamic economists, Muhammad Nejatullah Siddiqi, recently made an observation suggesting that it would not be possible to establish a *de novo* discipline of Islamic economics. The key, therefore, according to him lies in positioning Islamic vision in place of Anglo-Saxon economic vision (quoted by Kuran, 1995, p. 171). It seems to me, however, that the gospel of Islamic economics is very much alive in Pakistan. It is my contention, in this context, that the social goals emphasized by the Islamic economists are no different from the objectives as enunciated in the critiques of the neoclassical economics.

This chapter offers a brief summary of the neoclassical system, with special reference to microeconomics, followed by a discussion of its critiques, and then an examination of the claim of Islamic economics as a separate discipline.

The Neoclassical System[1]

The neoclassical theory differs from classical economics in that the main focus in this theory is on the market system. The classical tradition—as indeed the Marxian analysis— both put emphasis on long-run development, on the ownership of property [known as property rights] and on the distribution of income among those who have taken part in productive activity [the factors of production]. In the world of the neoclassical economics, however, these grand themes fade into the background [*ceteris paribus*, i.e. assumed as given].

Market exchange and allocation of resources is the central theme of the neoclassical theory. The resources are scarce and they are capable of alternative uses. The consumer follows his rational choice and maximizes his satisfaction as between competing demands. The producer also maximizes his profits by producing at a minimum cost and by receiving signals from the market about what to produce, how much to produce and for whom. Market is not necessarily a place in this analysis; it is a process of economic activity. Its purpose is to meet the demands [the ability to fulfil wants] of the consumer. It is also referred to as the system of consumer sovereignty.

Alfred Marshall was one of the pioneers of neoclassical economics and his approach came to be known as the Marshallian partial equilibrium analysis. [It was partial because the focus was on one aspect of the problem at a given time. For example, assuming income as given, how the demand reacts to the changes in price. It deals with equilibrium because the emphasis is on stability, i.e. supply and demand must interact to clear the market. That makes the market efficient.] It is a system in which costs and benefits correspond to each other and there are no externalities (i.e. the producer has caused no indirect problems such as pollution for which he claims no responsibility and which would indicate the *real* costs as being much higher if the pollution was taken into account). As neoclassical economics developed, it moved away from the Marshallian partial equilibrium analysis to the Walrasian model.

Leon Walras approached the neoclassical economics as a pure science. Marshall made an attempt to deal with practical problems, pushing his 'pure' theoretical ideas to footnotes and appendices. Walrasian objective was to establish a general equilibrium in which there was interdependence of all economic activity. With reference to a model of a simple economy, with two individuals and two goods, he made an effort to present a forceful argument for establishing a *positive* economic science (i.e. neutral concerning social issues). The importance of this point of view is discussed in the next section. The Walrasian system became quite suitable for simultaneous equations and other mathematical manipulations.

The next step in this structure is significant. The market becomes Pareto optimum when the welfare of an individual cannot be increased without at the same time creating a decrease in the welfare of the other individual. An important condition of optimality is that preferences of individuals are taken by themselves. Thus the social outcomes are derived from subjective preferences and with initial endowment as given. This analysis is similar to the Walrasian simple model and it assumes that an individual when he is guided only by his *personal* preferences of how much of good *a* in his possession he would be willing to give up in exchange for more of the good *b* in possession of the second person, he would reach a stable exchange with the other individual. If he now manages to acquire more of good *b* so that his gain corresponds to the loss incurred by the other individual for having less of that good, the market reaches a new equilibrium. A question arises what is the purpose of this simple argument which has exercised a very important influence in economic thinking. Behind the facade of simplicity, its political message is clear. When two individuals meet to *voluntarily* conduct an exchange, it is a voluntarily *agreed* transaction and it is *acceptable* to both parties. Thus, the free market results in the *optimum* condition. In other words, when the markets are left to their own mechanism, they create results which are best for all concerned. The limitations of this theorem are discussed in the next section.

The neoclassical theory, therefore, is a theory of voluntary exchange and efficient resources, and the neoclassical political economy becomes the instrument to achieve this goal. The main function of the state, then, is limited to the correction of market failures in the framework of the assumptions of the theory.

The Critiques of the Model

The neoclassical theory and its political economy are the dominant paradigms of modern times. There is, however, a growing list of critiques of its main assumptions and conclusions. I will select some points from this list which seem to me to be most relevant for my discussion. First, contrary to its claim, the neoclassical theory is not value-free. The market model is constructed in such a way that social intervention becomes a disturbing element creating inefficiency in the allocation of resources and the pattern of output of goods (Anderson 1980: 23–4). The model of course is positive in its approach and it has the scientific qualities, the positivists argue, because whatever extra-scientific judgements may creep into the choice of facts by an economist, the self-correcting mechanism of the social science eliminates bias as a result of free exchange and responsible criticism of ideas by other economists (Langé 1945: 22).

The problem, however, is that the basic material with which the economist deals is significantly different from that of the natural science. It is safe to assume, therefore, that economist *qua* economist makes value judgements in the discussion and application of economic theory (Dwyer 1981). The economist may claim in defence of his epistemology that his duty is to search interesting truths, to relieve doubt as well as to attain truth, and that he is not concerned with attaining truth *simpliciter* (Dwyer 1982: 82). He may also argue that he cannot keep his scientific neutrality if he takes into consideration social implications of his conclusions. In other words, he can maintain his objectivity only if his hypotheses are accepted on the basis of relevant empirical evidence, not some socio-political considerations. The choice of his data, however, is not like identifying facts in natural sciences and is open to value judgement, but to recognize the possibility of the economist's prejudice is not tantamount to epistemological anarchism (Dwyer: 92ff); it only underlines the fact that he must seek valuable truth, so that both the potential epistemic and pragmatic costs of mistakenly accepting some hypotheses may be recognized.

Secondly, the a priori assumption about the pursuit of self-interest as a dominant fact in human nature is not an evident and incontrovertible fact. This assumption is generally linked with the name of Adam Smith. Amartya Sen believes that Smith's economic analysis has been widely misinterpreted. It is prudence, Smith argued, which influences conduct of majority of people. And, it is not accurate to identify prudence with self-interest, because prudence is the union of the two qualities of reason and understanding, on the one hand, and self command on the other (Sen 1987: 22–5). Sen makes a persuasive point, and it seems that Smith was fully aware of the fact that pursuit of affluence would erode real tranquillity and he made a plea for 'humble security and contentment.' However, he thought that the ill effects of the tendency to acquire riches were mainly psychological. He completely lost sight of its social consequences (Roy 1992: 376).

In its general equilibrium analysis, the neoclassical economics makes maximization of utility (i.e., the satisfaction derived from the consumption of goods), the core of its theory. With the tools of analysis such as rational choice and by means of assumptions as to what goes into the utility function of the economic agent, the economist has turned economics from a logic of choice to a science of human behaviour. A renowned economist, Kenneth Arrow, suggests that his discipline's assumption about consumer rationality has in fact no basis in psychology and other allied fields (Arrow 1982: 1–9). And with respect to choice, the neoclassical economics seems to have failed to recognize that human beings when they emerge from their 'broken totality'—the phrase used by Roy with reference to Sartre (Roy 1992: 373)—they are capable of making diverse choices and decisions both material and non-material.

The model also assumes that the purpose of the market mechanism is to satisfy consumer demand. Some economists such as Sidney Schoeffler acknowledge that tastes may change over time and when they do the economists may have difficulty deciding conclusively about the level of well-being with the new tastes as compared with the first set of tastes (Schoeffler 1952: 883–7). While he expects biology to shed light on the phenomenon, he believes that the assumption remains valid. Lancaster has tried to solve the problem by defining it away as he argues that utility is derived from the characteristics of the goods, not the goods themselves. And this approach has been widely accepted by the economists (Lancaster 1966: 149–50).

The institutional economists such as J.K. Galbraith point out how the sovereignty of the consumer is replaced by that of the producer when product design and advertising as realities of modern capitalism are taken into account

(Galbraith 1958, 4th edn. 1984; 1967, 4th edn. 1985). The radical critics argue that the factors which affect consumption from outside the realm of economics—power relations—determine the pattern of consumer behaviour, which include distribution of property as well as experience in the basic sphere of social activity through work, education, culture, and environment (Amin 1993: 20; Gintis 1972).

The discounting of the future (to prefer present consumption to that in the future) which is an essential assumption of the model seems to be an obvious psychological law determining individual behaviour. Nevertheless, it cannot be extended to society at large as a universal phenomenon. It may not, for example, enter into the calculations of a peasant landowner because he might want to leave his children a means of making a living. If he discounted his future, he would have little incentive to maintain his landed capital and to upgrade its long term potential (Amin 1993: 22).

Economics and Ethics

The neoclassical model claims maximum attainable economic efficiency and social welfare. Any state action, therefore, in the market mechanism per se would be an interference in this goal. However, if and when there are real market failures the neoclassical political economy advocates suitable public policy to correct these failures. This is consistent with its purported value-neutral approach to economic behaviour.

The economy, for example, fulfils the criteria of Pareto optimum when no single individual in the exchange can be made better off without at the same time making the other individual worse off. The Paretian condition is based on a simple summation of individual values, but when there are more than two goods the issue of the formation of consumer preferences arises, which the Paretian model was not able to handle satisfactorily. It ignores, therefore, important ethical considerations such as the nature of consumer demand, or whether the 'economic man' provides the best approach to human behaviour (Sen 1987: 16). Human beings have a plurality of motivations, as referred to in the previous section, which are blithely assumed away in the positive analysis. Moreover, the market mechanism as noted above, is in large part a want-creating phenomenon, and it raises serious questions about whose goals the economic system serves and the ultimate purpose of economic activity (Dwyer 1982). It seems, therefore, that the market cannot be the final arbiter of social optimality. It would require that the choices, whether of action, institutions, motivations, or rules, etc., be ultimately determined by the goodness of the consequent state of affairs (Sen 1987: 39).

Pareto optimality ignores the distributional problem, because the exchange may in fact take place between an impoverished person and a rich individual. The neoclassical economics has taken the position until recently that rules specifying property rights may be important but they are outside the scope of its analysis. However, '[a] state can be Pareto optimum with some people in extreme poverty and others rolling in luxury so long as the miserable cannot be made better off without cutting into the luxury of the rich.' Thus, Pareto optimality can, like 'Caesar's Spirit', 'come hot from hell' (Sen: 32), and the neoclassical model gets trapped into its own utility concept. The challenge from outside the field of economics, such as the contribution of John Rawls to the theory of justice, has further underlined the dilemma of Pareto optimality. Rawls argues persuasively that there are criteria other than that of utility and that society can be made better off as long as transfer of income to the poor from the rich relatively increases the welfare of the former (Rawls 1971).

The neoclassical model continues to be quite tenacious. The Coase theorem, for example, tries to tackle two questions at the same time, that of property rights and of externalities (Coase 1960). In the ideal situation, the market costs and benefits are equal and if there are third party effects outside of the price system they are duly compensated and charged (Rhoads 1985: 113). A negative externality such as pollution, however, imposes a cost on outside agents causing pollution and the firm is able to produce more than it would if the cost of pollution was borne by it. Similarly, a positive externality would lead to a sub-optimal level of output. The economics of welfare of the Pigou tradition would resolve the issue through fines and subsidies, thus justifying state action (Pigou 1952).

Coase argues that given a structure of non-attenuated property rights and zero transaction costs, the problem of externalities does not exist, regardless of the distribution of property rights. If, for example, a farmer enjoyed exclusive property rights neighbouring those of a rancher, it would be in the best interests of the rancher to bribe the farmer to allow his cows to stray occasionally into his farm as long as the value of the marginal cow exceeds the value of the marginal crop loss. [In simple language, if the damage done by the cow is greater than the value of the crop in question, then the rancher would be induced to dispose of his cow.] This additional cost will induce the rancher to reduce his herd and for the farmer to increase his crop, thus restoring a value maximizing level of production. So, according to this theorem, the market process works superbly well, as usual.

Coase's example depends on the 'private' system of property rights and on the role of self-interest in market mechanism. If departure from self-interest can be systematically admitted into the economic analysis, the incentive problem may have to be reformulated (Sen: 89). Also, there may be a case for communal property rights and the so-called 'tragedy of commons' (in plain language, this phrase may be used to refer to a situation where a shared responsibility is not taken seriously and it leads to deterioration) may be irrelevant in a village economy where common property combined with private rights may prove to be both efficient and equitable (Runge 1986). The transaction costs [costs which are incurred in effecting market activity such as negotiation costs, in this case], moreover, may not be zero as assumed by Coase, and the social norms may consider the issue of property rights and distribution of property more than mere parameters that affect economic behaviour.

The question of public goods, similarly is examined in the neoclassical theory in terms of cost-benefit analysis. In its narrow approach used by the theory there is a grudging recognition that there may be a place for public goods by virtue of their indivisibility and diffuseness. However, there is strong support for market solution for most, if not all, of the goods included in this category, and it is argued that the free-rider problem [it arises when an individual can derive benefits without paying for them] can be resolved by means of a clear definition of property rights. It is not impossible, according to this approach for a lighthouse to be privately owned and operated (Nelson 1976, Coase 1974).

The ethical issue remains unresolved in spite of the abstract arguments about property rights. The initial allocation of property rights which would allow the economic agents to play their role is not easy to determine. The society also may take a broader view of costs and benefits in the production of a public good. It can be argued that from an ethical point of view one should contribute towards education even long after one's own children have left the system to join the labour force.

The Coase theorem cannot resolve the issue of externalities and public goods because of its highly restrictive assumptions. The neoclassical theory continues to face a real dilemma regarding its core argument of perfect competition. In the real world, moreover, production takes place under conditions of imperfect competition, and there is no firm small enough to face a perfectly elastic demand curve and produce homogeneous goods. (These two conditions, essential to the model of perfect competition, assume that a producer does not have a direct effect on the market price.) The focus in the neoclassical political economy is on public policy to control cartels, collusions and monopolies. Nevertheless, the claim for an invisible hand producing market efficiency is seriously damaged. Large corporations (Adam Smith attacked their ancestor, the joint-stock company) may exert political influence and product differentiation may permit them to control markets for their products. The result will be that the political system will not remain entirely neutral and the consumer might become a victim of managerial serfdom, a fate somewhat different from what Hayek warns concerning bureaucratic centrism (Hayek 1944), but quite insalubrious on the criteria of the neoclassical system. The criteria under the circumstance would shift from efficiency to what the consumer 'wants' as determined by the media message. The test of success then becomes profit maximization, not efficiency and profits.

In the new world of corporations, self interest is redefined. In the culture of contentment (Galbraith 1992: 80–88), to take the example from the world's dominant US economy, the market system is synonymous with freedom to pursue profit maximization by all means made available by the electronic media. The economist accommodates this culture by reaffirming his commitment to *laissez-faire,* and a minimum role for the government. There are a few exceptions, of course, which are recognized such as rescue for failing financial institutions. In this culture of contentment, the central bank would pursue policies which would bestow heavy rewards to the influential segments in the community of contentment (Galbraith 1992: 96).

The Islamic Economics

In the modern reconstruction of Islamic thought, the fundamental issue is whether Islam offers a detailed system of political economy, or whether its role as a religion is to establish criteria to assess and determine actions and practices of the government and the commmunity at large. Islamic economics belongs to the former category. It is defined as 'a social science which studies the economic problems of a people imbued with the values of Islam' (Mannan 1986: 18). It is a plea for the role of normative values in economic analysis. However, the definition raises two fundamental questions. First, as a social science, Islamic economics must have its own methodology and, second, that it offers a unique value system. I propose to examine both these questions in the following discussion.

Economics as a modern subject has its antecedents in the classical European tradition. For Adam Smith, it was a study in the nature and causes of wealth of nations. His *Wealth of Nations* is a treatise-tract because it integrates descriptive and prescriptive elements, positive and normative economics (Wright 1992: 60; Myrdal 1969: Chap. 1). He referred to his discipline as political economy. For Alfred Marshall, the subject matter of economics was a scientific inquiry in ordinary business of life and that its normative side should take a secondary position to its main purpose (Marshall 1920: 36). For this reason, he preferred the term economics over to political economy.

With Lionel Robbins, the positive aspect of economics was further reconfirmed as a science which studies behaviour for putting scarce means to alternative uses. The modern neoclassical tradition is characterized by the objective of exploring and expanding frontiers of knowledge in certain technical areas and in applying the knowledge to the problems of the society. As mentioned in the previous section, this is the mainstream tradition in the subject. The critics of this tradition continue to use the term political economy either to emphasize the relation between economics and public policy (Buchanan and Tullick 1962, Mueller 1979), or to challenge the mainstream theory with reference to institutional and historical constraints in the society (Mermelstein 1973, Katouzian 1980, especially pp. 182–3). In the former category, the economists employ the basic assumptions of economic theory and examine the interaction of state and market in national economic policy and international economic relations (Wright 1990). In the latter group, the distinction between the positive and the normative is discarded completely (Mermelstein 1973, Myrdal 1969).

Marxian economics is a complete antithesis of neoclassical theory and its assumptions often seem to influence the radical tradition in political economy. Marxism is in fact a theory of capitalism and its ideas are not in good health in the mainstream theory but they are alive and reasonably well in other areas such as history, sociology, and philosophy. Neoclassical and marxist economics both strive towards increasing social well-being. That is where they part company. Marxism rejects harmony of interests as assumed by neoclassicals. Value for Marx is a social relationship and, unlike neoclassical economics which extends its model to cover all possible societies, Marx emphasizes the historical relationship of the concept, and for him it is valid only for a capitalist society (Desai 1979: 10–11). The worker produces wealth under compulsion of the capitalist but obtains no benefit from the income created by the productive power. The rest of Marx's analysis and his predictions follow in the framework of these points.

Islamic economics claims to be a third and a better option to both Marxism and the neoclassical theory. It ignores the critiques of the neoclassical system which seems paradoxical. A major part of the literature under this title is concerned with macroeconomic policies from the point of view of what the Islamic economists believe are the basic injunctions of Islam about riba and payment of *zakat*. All this is discussed in the framework of applied neoclassical analysis and is based on the marginalist perspective of the pure market economy. In order to accommodate the role of the state, the criteria developed in welfare economics are incorporated in these discussions.[2]

From the epistemological point of view, Islamic economics does not offer a distinct logical structure of its own. The axioms which are presented as alternative to the mainstream economics correspond to the arguments in the critiques of the neoclassical theory. Let me summarize my arguments as follows:

a) Ends and Means: Islamic economists suggest that consumer demand in an Islamic economy will be restricted to those goods which are not forbidden according to the religion. As for the means to fulfil demands, some Islamic economists challenge the concept of scarcity as contrary to Islam. Relevant Qur'anic verses such as 6:136 and 7:10 are invoked to suggest that God has created means for the material fulfilment of man's life. Obviously, it is a gross misunderstanding of the concept of scarcity, because the basic economic fact is that, given the endowment, supply of goods in one category cannot be increased without taking resources away from the production of other goods. The question of abundance then sometimes is resolved by suggesting that the Islamic basket of goods requires the condition of appropriateness of production (Choudhury 1992: 19–20).

In general, the Islamic economists accept the concept of scarcity and are quite content with invoking welfare criteria in resolving the question of waste in the economy.

b) Self-interest: It is suggested that the Islamic man will temper his self-interest with considerations of rewards and retributions in the hereafter. He will be guided by his faith in *tahwid* (divine, oneness) and *adl* (equity or justice) in his spiritual pursuits in tandem with his economic well being. These attributes along with free will and responsibility will make it possible for the Islamic economy to function in a superior manner than that assumed in the positivist approach of the neoclassical economics (Naqvi 1981b: 45–57; 1994: 24–34; Chapra 1992: 202ff). As noted in the section above the critics of the neoclassical model do not accept the assumption that self-interest alone drives human beings.

c) Property rights: The neoclassical theory has on the whole ignored the issue of property rights, taking it as an exogenous factor, not interfering with the functioning of the market. However, as already referred to above, it has become the focus of attention concerning the role of non-attenuated property rights with reference to externalities and public goods. The Islamic economists are unanimous in their view that ownership of property belongs to God (Behdad 1992). In other words, individual rights could be abrogated or restricted in an Islamic state, depending upon whether the criteria to interpret this Islamic injunction are based on populist or public control approaches (Behdad: 80–84). In the real world, this statement has only a rhetorical significance, as the Objectives Resolution was supposed to have when it was first introduced in the Constituent Assembly. In general, Muslim countries recognize the right to private property and the state provides legal machinery to settle private disputes concerning property ownership, hoarding practices, and excess profits. Moreover, the tradition in the Islamic jurisprudence has been explicitly in favour of non-attenuated property rights in land and capital (Behdad: 96)

d) Competition: It is assumed that the Islamic economy will be based on the principle of competition, within the norms of fairness and justice in accordance with Islam. In order to fulfil these two conditions, the criteria of Pareto optimality will not be central to Islamic economics (Naqvi 1981a, 1994: 60), and this departure from the neoclassical model is presented as a distinct characteristic of Islamic economics. However, as pointed out by Sen, the ethical content of the welfare implications of Pareto optimality are rather modest and it is an extremely limited way of assessing social achievement (Sen 1994: 35). The role of the firm in establishing equilibrium in an Islamic economy is not clearly defined. Pleasure of God is an essential constraint on the behaviour of the producer. Some economists suggest the importance of Islamic brotherhood in this regard. Both these factors create a real dichotomy in the market, and the Islamic economists end up following the neoclassical tools of economic analysis with a caveat for ethical Islamic rhetoric (Nomani and Rehnema 1994: 95).

The Islamic economists argue that given the assumption of *tawhid* and *adl*, existence of monopoly is not possible in an Islamic economy. The real issue, however, is not about monopoly as such but imperfect competition which is a ubiquitous phenomenon caused by production of brand name goods, and oligopolistic practices. It occurs when product differentiation can be easily introduced and it relies mainly on the role of technology and cost curves, so that production takes place at a clearly suboptimal point. The profit-and-loss sharing as a preferred business organization for the Islamic economy does not tackle this phenomenon at all.

Conclusion

The methodology of Islamic economics is based on the assumption that the market system can be made to function better for the common good when the economic agents are influenced by Islamic values. This approach is seriously flawed for several reasons. First, religious zeal cannot correct the imperfections in the market which arise mainly owing to the internal mechanism of the economy. The model of perfect competition adjusted to accommodate the *homo-Islamicus* does not solve this problem.

The market mechanism based on rational self-interest as defined in the neoclassical theory creates serious social tensions in the economic system. One such tension occurs when there is an imbalance between material goods and positional goods (Hirsch 1978). As the economy grows the positional goods may not increase corresponding to the supply of material goods and the economy may tend to focus on the needs of minority elite groups for higher education, travel, vacations, suburban living, etc. Therefore, as the general prosperity grows, the role of redistributive mechanism becomes important. This would be possible only if the individualistic ethic is tempered by an adequate degree of altruism, something akin to Rawlsian system of justice. Some Islamic economists advocate a *shuratic* process for deciding the allocation of resources for the economy as a whole so that individual agents are free to pursue their objectives based on *tawhid* and *adl*, subject to this constraint (Choudhury 1992b).[3]

The argument is fallacious because it is in conflict with the market economy which they support. The controlling authority would suffer from a serious handicap for not having the relevant information at its disposal, for decision making at such a large scale. Any mechanism of planning, as envisaged in that system, would suffer from what may be called bureaucratic inertia. The micro-order in the market, as a rule, responds relatively quickly to shifts in supply and demand, leading to socially useful results (Heilbroner 1192: 80). Under some conditions, however, market outcomes would be clearly disequilibrating, such as speculative activity in the future grain prices (Heilbroner 1992: 84), or in the foreign exchange market. State intervention in selected areas of the economy, therefore, would provide a balance in the market mechanism, accompanied by a sense of ethic on the part of the individual players.

What role religion can play in this context is a difficult question. The place of religious ethic in the rise of capitalism remains a controversial issue. Religion may be invoked to foster a moral sense, to succeed in this world or to abnegate material needs in favour of spiritual salvation. Whether it is the dogma which attracts certain types of people, or vice versa, has not been established as a clear relationship. In general, it would be difficult to argue that people should do what is right only to avoid the wrath of God (J. Robinson 1964: 14). In the case of Islam which has an elaborate code of conduct from daily prayers to the annual month of fasting, the argument that the practice of religion would necessarily lead to a certain of altruistic sense required for an ethical economic system is highly tenuous, both in theory and on the basis of reality. As often observed by sociologists, people have a tendency to compartmentalize their belief and the demands of their practical life. And, religious rituals become a proxy for a true sense of moral behaviour.

The economic system in which micro-order flourishes has close correspondence with the political system suitable for this order. It is a duality of realms with smudgy boundaries, a social order at once divided and united, motivated by different imperatives that sometimes agree and sometimes do not easily coexist (Heilbroner: 49–54). What the duties of each realm should be is a question which has not been given any serious attention by either the Islamic economists or the advocates of the Islamic state. The market system even in the most advanced societies is not as open as they seem to claim. The economy, whether it is based on the *laissez-faire* principle or whether it works under the umbrella of welfare constraints, is usually driven by unequal power relations among the capitalists, and between capital and labour. In the feudal agrarian sector of a developing country such as Pakistan, the main features of the command system continue to thrive and flourish. It may be argued, in this context, that Islamic economics creates a scapegoat for the shortcomings of government policies (Nasr 1989). It is easy, for example, to introduce the Sharia Act with great fanfare, as the government of Pakistan did in 1991; it is equally as difficult to come up with a meaningful legislation for such issues as land reform in the country. There is another problem with Islamic economics and that relates to its concept of distributive system. It may not be as effective as claimed to be, and may even have some regressive effects on the economy. All this is complicated by the fact that the relation between the two realms is facing a new challenge in which capital is becoming dedomiciled and the global economy is turning into a global village.

NOTES

1. This and the next section broadly follows the usual textbook approach. *See,* for example, Edwin Mansfield: *Microeconomics: Theory and Applications,* New York and London, Norton, 1970; James A. Caporaso and David P. Levine: *Theories of Political Economy,* New York, Cambridge University Press, 1992.

2. The idealized notion of equity and justice as derived from the Qur'an becomes the basis of the economic system. Individual freedom is guaranteed within the framework of the two criteria. Some refer to this system as Islamic welfare economics, and they emphasize that it is not the mean between socialism and capitalism, 'but is symptomatic of a general philosophy which abhors unnatural extremist behaviour at individual and collective levels' (Naqvi 1981a: 79). Others build up their arguments for social economics and from that premise Islamic economics is considered as a natural step forward (Choudhury 1986).

3. The shuratic system will consist of a system of councils of ulama as well as representatives of government labour, business, and education. *See also,* review of Choudhury's book by Sohrab Behdad in the Middle East Studies Association, *Bulletin,* December, 1993 pp. 197–8.

CHAPTER 3

The Question of *Riba*[1]

The Qur'anic injunctions against *riba* are clear and categorical. Opinions differ, however, about the meaning of riba and the scope of the injunctions in the context of a modern industrial society. The early Islamic jurists used the term in a broad sense, in order to emphasize the problem of unlawful gains and unearned income derived from the use of money, barter and exchange. The advocates of the Islamic state in Pakistan have focused almost entirely on the problem of credit and loans, and it is their view that all pre-arranged and fixed charges on the use of capital should be eliminated. This view is one of the crucial foundations on which Islamic economics is built.[2]

The objectives of Islamicization include compulsory collection of *zakat* and implementation of the laws of inheritance, but the fundamental goal is to establish a just monetary system by eliminating *riba* as interpreted by the traditionalist ulama. Interest-free banking was introduced in Pakistan in 1988 under the rule of General Ziaul Haq. For the ulama of the country, it was only a modest step in the right direction. The Sharia Act coveted their support in May 1991 by providing for a commission to 'oversee the process of elimination of *riba* from every sphere of economic activity in the shortest possible time...' (Human Rights Commission of Pakistan, *Newsletter*, July 1991). In November 1991, the Federal Shariat Court completely ignored the proposed commission in the Sharia Act, and in a sweeping judgement it declared that all laws relating to interest were repugnant according to the Qur'an and *Sunna* and, instructed the government to bring these laws in conformity with the injunctions of Islam, as interpreted by the Court, by 30 June 1992 (Key Law Reports, 1992: 176). The Shariat Court, in fact, was acting with reference to various petitions challenging the provisions for charging of interest in twenty acts, statutes, and orders as listed in its judgement, and they included The Interest Act of 1839, The State Bank of Pakistan Act of 1956, and Banking Companies (Recovery of Loans) Ordinance, 1979. These pieces of legislation together form an important link between the citizen and the financial institution with regard to his rights and obligations in these agreements. The Court decided, however, that these rights and obligations were not a matter of direct concern for it, as its jurisdiction according to the constitution extended to a question of higher importance, that of repugnancy of laws to the injunctions of Islam (Key Law Reports: 166).

It is obvious that the judgement of the Shariat Court could not have been implemented without causing a massive confusion in the economy. The ruling of the Court remains in abeyance but the question will continue to shadow the political economy of Pakistan until the two questions concerning the role of Islam and the reconstruction of religious thought in Islam are not resolved with reference to Pakistan. The Shariat Court's ruling, it seems, was based on an unbalanced and one-sided argument. The Government of Pakistan was represented by a group of senior counsels in the court proceedings. Their submission in defence of the claim that modern interest did not fall in the category of riba did not seem to be accurately informed by the relevant literature on the subject. Their submission included a list of seven contributions, one of them being from Fazlur Rahman, MA, of Muslim University, Aligarh, whose views seemed to contradict the position of the counsels. In any case, the court rejected these contributions except that of Fazlur Rahman whose argument was endorsed with approval by it. If the counsels had intended to draw attention of the court to Professor Fazlur Rahman, whose article is discussed below, then it was the case of a regrettable mistaken identity.

The position of the chief justice of the court on this issue was well known. In his capacity as chairman of the Council of Islamic Ideology, appointed by General Ziaul Haq, he had directed a report making recommendations for interest-free banking in Pakistan. All the main references in the court proceedings in support of the traditional arguments about *riba* were to this report, and to some Islamic scholars holding similar views.

The debate on the question of *riba* was started during the period of President Ayub Khan. It is in this period that traditional interpretation of *riba* was challenged in the country. The 1962 Constitution proclaimed by Ayub Khan in his capacity as the military ruler formally set the stage for a modernist position. In the section on Principles of Policy it enunciated that '*riba* (usury) shall be eliminated', thus using the parenthesis to define 'riba' (Safdar Mahmud: 513). In 1963, Professor Fazlur Rahman [d.1988] published an article in Urdu offering a new meaning of *riba* (Fazlur Rahman 1963. For references given here *see*, Fazlur Rahman 1964). Four years later, an ex-Auditor General Of Pakistan, Syed Yaqub Shah (d.1977), produced a book in which he argued that the purpose of the Qur'anic prohibition of *riba* was to ban usury in the economy (Syed Yaqub Shah 1967). He had been writing on the subject since the early 1950s and also corresponding with various ulama, including Abul A'la Maudoodi (d.1979), the then head of the Jama'at-e-Islami. Maudoodi published an enlarged and revised edition of his book *Sood* in 1961, reasserting the traditional view on *riba* (Maudoodi 1961, references are from the 1984 reprint). The book originally appeared in 1948 and was based on his articles in his monthly *Tarjumanul Qur'an* written during 1936–7 in Hyderabad (Deccan), India. Two of the three appendices in the revised edition of the book deal with the questions raised by Syed Yaqub Shah and the Idara-e-Saqa'fat-e-Islamia of which he was an active member. Supporting Maudoodi's position, Anwar Iqbal Qureshi had already written a book in English on the eve of the partition of British India, and it received renewed interest in this period (Anwar Iqbal Qureshi 1946).

There is no reference to the article of Professor Fazlur Rahman on this issue in the court proceedings, as noted above. Concerning Syed Yaqub Shah, his article on the topic of productive credit was included by the counsels for the Government of Pakistan in their submission. In its rebuttal of Syed Yaqub Shah, the court also refers to another of his contributions in Urdu on the question of interest on commercial loans, but his book is not mentioned at all.

In this chapter, I propose to survey the above four contributions as they have a common link in the debate on the issue. This will be followed by a discussion of how the classical jurists faced the practical problems created by the Qur'anic injunction against *riba*. My purpose is to emphasize that the role of interest as envisaged in a competitive economy is not incompatible with Islamic justice.

Maudoodi on *Riba*

The contributions of Maudoodi on Islamic law and jurisprudence are well known throughout the Islamic world. He wrote in Urdu but his publications are available in many other languages. His writings and ideas are of special significance in Pakistan because, as head of the Jama'at-e-Islami, he was able to exert considerable influence on the politics of the country.

The relevant Qur'anic verses which prohibit *riba* are ar-Rum (30:39), al-'Imran (3:130), and al-Baqara (2:274–80).

In *ar-Rum,* a moral declaration is passed against *riba.* In the second sura, *riba* is defined as continued redoubling of the loan and is categorically prohibited. In the third set of verses, there is a clear warning to those who may practice *riba* under the guise of *bay'* (trading), and the believers are asked to relinquish whatever remained due from *riba* and take the principle only.

In the chapter entitled 'The Islamic laws concerning *riba*' (Maudoodi 147–61), Maudoodi focuses on the verses of *ar-Rum* and *al-Baqara* and emphasizes that the phrase *al-riba* as used in these verses refers to the practice of money-lending that was well known among Arabs of the Jahilia period. The main task, therefore, is to describe the practice and to examine the historical evidence regarding the matter. He draws the conclusion from his discussion that *riba* is that fixed and prearranged amount on the use of capital which is claimed by the lender. He calls it *riba al-nasi'a* (loan transaction). It is also referred to as the Qur'anic *riba* in the literature on the subject in order to distinguish it from the concept of *riba al-fazl* —the *riba* of the sunnah of the Prophet. Maudoodi discusses this concept in a separate chapter entitled 'The Adjuncts of *Sood*' (pp.163–82). According to this concept, *riba* may arise when in exchange of commodities there is an 'excess' in their countervalues. In the traditions of the Prophet this kind of possible excess refers to exchange of a given quantity of gold with another piece of unequal quality of the metal. Similarly for silver, barley, wheat, dates and salt. He notes that there are differences of opinion among the jurists concerning the scope of this *riba*: whether it is confined to the six commodities as mentioned in the traditions, or whether its purpose is to establish a general principle in all exchange transactions. He believes that the differences are really concerning the borderline cases, and that the purpose of declaring *riba al-fazl* as unlawful is to close the loophole in the practice of *riba* by broadening the scope of the Qur'anic injunctions against it.

In order to establish the modern context of the Qur'anic injunctions, Maudoodi offers a lengthy and somewhat repetitive discussion on the subject. His position, which he presents in a forceful manner, may be summarized as follows:

There is a negative and a positive aspect of the injunctions. In the former category are various arguments justifying interest as a risk taken by the lender, the opportunity for investment forgone, or rent on the use of capital (pp. 61–101). In view of the contractual agreement between the lender and the borrower, the question of risk becomes irrelevant, says Maudoodi. The main issue is whether the lender should be rewarded for time, and the answer is obviously in the negative. Also, the loanable fund in all likelihood represents a surplus over and above the needs of the lender. This surplus has no alternative uses for him. The charge for its use cannot be called rent, as some creditor would try in order to justify their activities, because rent applies to durable goods, and for the wear and tear of these goods (p. 67).

Maudoodi further elaborates his argument with reference to two areas of economic activity in which interest may play a role. A loan might be sought by an indigent person to meet his basic needs. In such a case interest would clearly represent an exploitation of the poor. When a loan, on the other hand, is made for productive use, the reward for the lender would be justified only if he shared the risk of the enterprise. In this context, Maudoodi focuses directly on the question of time preference and rejects the view that man by nature prefers the present to an uncertain future, and that he is willing to pay the price to fulfil his wants. However, even if this argument were to be accepted, it would still not be possible to determine a reasonable price which would bridge the gap between the present and the future. What is considered reasonable has been changing throughout history. As for the role of the market in determining interest, it is the capitalist who manipulates the supply of loanable funds and controls interest rates. Maudoodi also rejects the argument that interest encourages saving and that it facilitates mobilization of capital. Behind 'thrift' is in fact greed operating for accumulation of wealth, in fewer and fewer hands, consequently creating deficiency in the general purchasing power and leading to recession in the economy (p. 95).

What about the role of interest in the allocation of resources? Maudoodi believes that by emphasizing the rate of return on the use of capital as the sole criterion for investment, society might be deprived of its social needs. In a choice between a proposal for an affordable housing scheme and for building a structure for a movie theatre, the latter would win on the basis of comparative rates of return on investment (p. 98).

With regard to the positive aspects of the prohibition against *riba*, Maudoodi believes that the use of interest is detrimental to society as it encourages selfishness and greed; it creates social conflict and promotes international exploitation (pp. 102–118). With its focus on short term gains, the long term considerations are ignored; the owner of capital prefers to avoid having the loan tied for longer duration because the interest rate might change; consequently, the entrepreneur would try to maximize his advantage with existing equipment and would be discouraged from renewing and replacing his machine (p. 116).

To summarize, Maudoodi's position on *al-riba*, especially *riba al-nasi'a* is that there is no difference between the practice of moneylending that prevailed during the *Jahilia* period and the modern banking system. This is the basis of his claim concerning the scope of *riba* extending to interest as used in modern times. His discussion of the modern banking system, in fact, gives a clear indication of his thoughts on the subject (pp. 129–46). He traces the evolution of the institution from the goldsmith as depository of money to the period when money was based on the use of precious metals, to the birth of credit and fractional reserve system. In describing this historical development, he uses phrases such as deceit, trickery, deception, forgery, and fraud to underline the modern system. For him, it is the same old *mahajan* (a Hindi word for indigenous merchant banker of the Indian subcontinent during the British rule) under a new name, only more organized and able to expand his usual moneylending business with the help of depositors' funds.

Maudoodi was an erudite scholar of Islamic law and jurisprudence. His central point is that the owner of capital can claim a reward for the use of his capital from the realized profits only. Many of the arguments he offers in support of his claim, however, would appear to be naive to an economist, such as the public versus private needs in an interest-based economy, the iron grip of the lender on the financial market, and investment decisions concerning new equipment and the replacement of the old machines. The force of these arguments against the place of fixed reward for capital is at best tenuous, but they nevertheless raise pertinent questions about the workings of the present-day financial institutions. How stable, for example, is fractional reserve system? Or, how monopolistic are the modern banks? When we discuss these questions, we move from the realm of ethics of *riba* with reference to the early Islamic period to the ethics of *riba* in the context of the modern capitalist system, and to the mundane controversies about suitable economic policies for growth and stability as well as the new kinds of economic realities and the new kinds of economic offences. In this context, Maudoodi's position on the subject becomes largely irrelevant.

The significance of Maudoodi's contribution is that because of his dual role as an Islamic scholar and as head of a political organization he managed to draw attention to the narrow issue of *riba* versus interest at the expense of other, and perhaps equally important problems facing the Pakistan economy.

Anwar Iqbal Qureshi on *Riba*

Qureshi believes that it is not necessary to offer intellectual arguments in favour of the Qur'anic injunctions against *riba* (Qureshi 1946: 4). The question, however, is not about *riba* but about the definition of *riba*, and he does proceed with this task in spite of his assertion.

The main section of his book which deals with the Islamic theory of interest covers the familiar ground as summarized above with reference to Maudoodi (Qureshi pp. 44–122). He explains *riba al-nasi'a* in the framework of the relevant verses of the Qur'an and the traditions of the Prophet. He examines arguments such as justification of *riba* as a reward for opportunities forgone by the lender, with specific reference to the views of Imam Fakhrud-Din Razi. He notes the differences of opinion concerning the application of *riba al-fazl* to commodities other than six as mentioned in the traditions. On the basis of his discussion of the Islamic theory of interest, he concludes that there is no difference between *riba* as forbidden by the Qur'an and the modern bank interest. The only legitimate claim of the lender of capital is with regard to a share in the profits earned by the borrower, because profits are the result of joint participation and risk-taking.

Not all fixed and pre-arranged charges are prohibited, however, and rent falls in this category, according to Qureshi. His explanation about this difference is similar to that of Maudoodi, except that he makes an explicit comparison between loanable funds and rental charge. Rent from agricultural land, and rent on a house or another durable structure is justified as these goods do not retain their original shape, nature or character after use. On the other hand, money loaned for a given period is returned to the lender 'unimpaired', as well as the additional interest income (p. 114). How 'unimpaired' does the sum of money lent remain when it is returned to the creditor can only be determined after taking into consideration various factors including inflation, which Qureshi does not take into account.

With regard to the Western theories of interest, he concludes that none of these theories offers a satisfactory explanation as to why interest is paid (pp. 12–43). In his brief review of the ancient and the medieval periods, he notes that interest began to be tolerated as there was a gradual decline in the powers of the Church along with the rise of secular states. He finds considerable support in Keynes' views about the possibility of a zero rate of interest (p. 36), which Keynes envisaged if and when an economy reached a stage where it had abundance of capital.

Modern banks, for Qureshi are the moneylenders who have gained new respectability under the umbrella of the new institutional name (p. 141–2). Their activities directly contribute to business cycles and economic instability. Also, fixed interest rates exercise a very sinister influence on economic development. For example, in the early stages of British rule in India, the railway companies were guaranteed a minimum interest of five per cent per annum, but the income from their operation was lower than was expected, with the result that the government's railway budget suffered a huge deficit by 1869 (pp. 215–16).

The financing of public projects such as railways in British India during the nineteenth century is a very complex issue, however. It cannot be invoked by Qureshi in defence of his position on *riba*. Also, the entire principle of financial management, and scope of debt-equity ratio in major investments, has undergone drastic changes during the last century.

There is an implicit assumption in Qureshi's treatment of the subject that elimination of interest would also eliminate business cycles, but no clear or persuasive argument has been offered in this regard. While the industrial economies have been trying to deal with their booms and busts, their growth over the past hundred years has been quite impressive, and their financial institutions have played a significant role as intermediaries of growth.

There is a formal similarity between *riba* and modern interest. Both require contractual obligation to pay a fixed charge for the use of capital. Can both be regarded as similar in substance when the former is based on a binary relationship in which the moneylender uses his surplus capital almost exclusively in pursuit of this activity, but the other is determined by the market forces in which capital is capable of alternative uses, carrying with it its own risks and uncertainties?

Against the Mainstream: Fazlur Rahman

In a very lucid presentation, Fazlur Rahman argues that *riba* in the pre-Islamic days was based on the practice of doubling and redoubling the principle sum as penalty for failure to repay the loan on time. The verse *al-'Imran*, therefore, occupies a central place in the Qur'anic injunctions against *riba* (Rahman: p. 5). He says that the question of the chronological order of the verses and the historical context of their revelation is important in order to understand the issue. He also notes that the tradition ascribed to Caliph Umar—that the last verse to be sent down was on *riba* and that the Prophet had no time to expound it—has been contradicted by other traditions (p. 8). He concludes that the first verse about riba, *ar-Rum* (30:39), was revealed during the early years of the Prophet's Meccan life; the second verse, *al-'Imran* (3:130) was revealed after the Muslim defeat at Uhud, and preceded and followed by verses which analyze the cause of the defeat and its consequences; and the context of the verses 2:274–80 of *al-Baqara* is the period before the last Jewish tribe of Banu Qurayza was exiled (pp. 11–12).

Rahman defines *riba* as 'an exorbitant increment whereby capital sum is doubled several-fold against a fixed extension of the term of payment of debt' (p. 5). He rejects Maudoodi's assertion, therefore, that the Qur'anic *riba* is the excess money which is obtained on determinate conditions, and at fixed rate, in consideration of the period for which the money is lent. He points out that the literature on the traditions of the Prophet, which is the basis of Maudoodi's definition of *riba*, is contradictory and inconclusive (pp. 20–21). For example, it is reported according to one tradition that there is no *riba* except on loans; in another tradition it is said that *riba* does not occur when payment is made on the spot. However, according to another tradition, the hand-to-hand exchange must be 'like for like' in order to avoid *riba*. This particular tradition, says Rahman, is based on the concept of *riba* which must be a later innovation, as it was not known to the 'Eminent companions of the Prophet, like Mu'awiya...and Abd Allah b' Umar...' (p. 13).

The traditions concerning *riba al-nasi'a* and *riba al-fazl*, therefore, do not appear to be authentic, according to Rahman. However, he warns that it would be a folly to ignore their moral import. Following Ibn Qayyim and Rashid Riza, Fazlur Rahman concludes that the Qur'anic *riba* is the manifest *riba* (i.e. continued redoubling), which must be prohibited as a 'religious necessity' (p. 30). There are many other forms of unfair commercial practices which must also be recognized and dealt with through suitable social and economic policies.

Rahman explains how, in pre-Islamic Arabia, the practice of *riba* brought considerable hardship to borrowers who in most cases were destitute and needy persons. As time passed, the troubles of the debtor multiplied until his possessions and belongings were lost to the creditor. The creditor in this manner acquired by unlawful means the wealth of his brother (p. 34).

In the modern economy, however, interest rate occupies the same place in the market as other prices, that is to regulate the supply and demand of credit and to ration it among the customers. Maudoodi's denunciation of the banking system betrays his ignorance of the modern institution, says Rahman. He also notes that in the Communist school of thought it is labour and not capital that produces surplus value. 'On this theory, there is no basis at all even for the profits of private business, not to speak of the profits made by the banks or the bank-interest (p. 38).

The system of the economy which the Qur'an requires us to establish will be based on the spirit of cooperation and mutual consideration (*sadaqah*). The opposite of *riba* is not bay' but *sadaqah*. The juristic hair-splitting was substituted for the moral importance attached to the prohibition of *riba* because *riba* and *bay'* were considered as opposite to each other. There is a tension between *riba* and *sadaqah* of which *bay'* is quasi-middle term (pp. 31–2).

In order to establish a system of the economy which the Qur'an requires, the volume of wealth and capital in the country would have to be increased to such a point that equality or near equality comes to exist between supply and demand of money and credit. Until such a Welfare Cooperative Commonwealth of Islam is established, we cannot close our eyes to present realities. The possibilities for establishing such a Commonwealth are not bright, and in fact 'we are now at the opposite pole from the social order envisaged by the Qur'an' (p. 39).

The response of the ulama to the contribution of Fazlur Rahman was not to discuss his ideas but to denounce him or, if possible, to ignore his existence. The Shariat Court in its judgement, for example, claims that as far as the question of *riba al-nasi'a* is concerned, they have not come across any difference of opinion regarding its prohibition, and further that 'There is no commentator of the Holy Qur'an, nor narrator of *Ahadith,* and no jurist of Islamic fiqah worth the name who has even expressed or even mentioned any doubt regarding any obscurity or ambiguity in its meaning' (Key Law Reports, p. 85).

Rahman argues against what he calls manifest *riba* and accepts the role of interest in a *bay'*-oriented economy. However, he prefers the system which is based on cooperation (*sadaqah*). His pseudo-Keynesian musings on the possible abundance of capital when its marginal efficiency would fall to zero is a confirmation of his belief in the Islamic bliss which he admits seems to be receding far from the horizon.

Rahman was the first Islamic scholar of Pakistan who offered a bold modernist interpretation of *riba*. It was the first time that a leading scholar of Islam had argued the case cogently and comprehensively in light of the Qur'anic verses and the traditions of the Prophet. From the time of the Objectives Resolution, the question of bank interest had been at the forefront of Pakistani politics. His essay dealt with the issue, almost exclusively emphasizing the *riba al-nasi'a*, and keeping in view the position of Maudoodi on this matter which was shared by most other ulama. It was published a year after the 1962 Constitution was proclaimed by General Ayub Khan, in the atmosphere of a degree of optimism in the country, not experienced by the people since that time. As the political economy of Pakistan faltered and Ayub Khan's star got under the cloud of political intrigues and opposition, Fazlur Rahman became an easy target for Maudoodi and other ulama.

Another View Against the Mainstream

Syed Yaqub Shah started to examine the question of *riba* in the context of the pension fund to which he was to become entitled upon retirement. Maudoodi advised him to forgo interest on the fund (Maudoodi 1984: 264–73), which would be a large chunk of the total amount. He was assured by a couple of other ulama that his total provident fund including interest did not fall in the category of *riba*. It is a matter which, he says, prompted him to examine the entire issue.

His book is divided into fourteen chapters, ranging from a discussion of interest-based economies of Muslim countries to the question of insurance and *zakat*. Like Fazlur Rahman, Yaqub Shah believes that the Qur'anic injunction is against a special kind of practice of 'continued redoubling' of the usurious charge on loans by the poor and needy. Unlike Rahman, however, he is of the view that *riba* refers only to loans for consumption purposes which 'in most cases' would include the poor but would not necessarily be confined to them. The reference in the Qur'an to *al-riba* was to a practice with which the Arabs of the pre-Islamic period were quite familiar. The exact details of the practice, however, have not been recorded accurately by the Islamic jurists and historians. The result is that all we have is the literal meaning of the term and how it has been interpreted in the classical jurisprudence (p. 38). He then quotes extensively from jurists such as Tabari, Razi, and Ibn Qayyim and, concludes that *riba* in *Jahilia* (Pre-Islamic Arab) was charged in consideration of extension of time, but he gives no other evidence in support of his statement (pp. 60–67).

This practice of *riba*, says Yaqub Shah, would not be suitable for the needs of trade (p. 68). He rejects therefore the views of writers such as H. Lammens (1924) that in the pre-Islamic Mecca there was a sophisticated financial system in which loans of all kinds were used. Maudoodi, however, believes that the Quraysh were strategically located, and that they were able to earn huge profits from their trade. For such a lucrative business, loans at a reasonable rate could not have been difficult to get (Maudoodi, op cit.: 296–300). It is important to add here that for Maudoodi *riba* includes any fixed and pre-arranged charge on loans; it need not be exorbitant.

Yaqub Shah discusses the concept of *riba al-fazl* and suggests that it is relevant only with regard to the old practice of barter trade.

He examines critically various objections to the role of interest in the economy, i.e. it promotes selfishness, or that it causes business cycles, and explains why the entrepreneur would prefer to use both debt and equity to finance his activity: debt would allow him to calculate his costs accurately and equity will give him prospects of better reward. (Equity may be distinguished from debt as the former is based on ordinary shares entitled to expectation of profit whereas the latter carries a fixed claim.) And that when an investor borrows capital, he does so on the basis of his calculations about the profitability of his enterprise; he takes a risk which is an essential part of his business. Similarly, the banks take risk in providing loans to investors, and serious defaults on the borrowed funds could affect the viability of a bank (p. 100).

The banks also provide an avenue for people with fixed income, including widows, pensioners, and orphans with the expectation of guaranteed earnings from their deposits. To accept a lower (discounted) but a certain rate of return as against a higher but an uncertain income is a reasonable choice, and the ulama have not been able to provide any convincing argument against it.

He concludes that interest on producer loans is not contrary to Islamic injunctions about *riba*. What needs to be emphasized is good banking practice in order to improve the financial system. For the economy as a whole, it is necessary to discourage possibilities of unearned income. For the (subsistence) farmers, and for the needs of the poor, a separate financial system will have to established (p. 209).

In an Islamic economy as envisaged by Syed Yaqub Shah, interest will play its usual role to allocate funds for all productive activities, as well as to facilitate government borrowings. And it will be paid on all deposits kept in banks. The only exception will be regarding the purchase of consumer goods, which will have to be financed by personal income and savings. Being an accountant by profession, he had no difficulty in arguing that the discount rate as an arithmetical concept related to the expected rate of return on investment did not fall in the category of *riba*. This is the crux of his main argument. He did not extend his argument, however, to include the modern economic phenomenon where the source of capital in an industrial society is different from that of the moneylender. In the market economy, as I have stated above, capital has alternative uses as between various productive activities as well as between consumption and production. In other words, interest is a price for use of capital and its cost for consumer loan as against the forgone alternative for its use for production can be easily calculated.

Fazlur Rahman defined *riba* in the context of the practice prevailing in the medieval economy but did not go into the details of uses of modern bank interest. Yaqub Shah struggled with this point, with reference to the fact that the Qur'anic verse uses the phrase *al-riba*, not *riba*, making it a specific kind of riba. This point is not crucial to his position on the issue.

The counsel for Pakistan, in his list of submissions to the Court had included a photocopy of the relevant argument of Yaqub Shah from his short essay on Islam and productive credit. The Shariat Court focused on this particular item, ignoring all other writings of Yaqub Shah and suggested that relying on the prefix 'al' was absurd— '...only an ignorant man will say so' and further that the use of interest for loans including commercial loans was a fact of history. In spite of this assertion, however, the historical record is murky and subject to interpretation.

To Recapitulate

There is a definite support for creating an interest-free economy in Pakistan. Many professional Pakistanis, for example, may not feel as categorical about *sood* and *riba* as the ulama do, but they experience occasional ambivalence about the problem. In July 1956, an economist of international stature, Professor Harry Johnson (d. 1977), conducted a refresher course in economics for bureaucrats in Karachi. He was faced with this issue during the course of the seminar discussions and suggested that the market principle must be distinguished from considerations of social justice, and that '...the view that interest is a bad thing is economically nonsensical (unless it is a merely terminological dispute) until the economy has reached a stage at which no more capital can be usefully employed (Johnson 1962: 159).

There is also a very strong moral sentiment about interest as indicated by the term *sood* and related phrases such as *soodkhar* and *sood-khor* (those who eat *sood*), and those who practice it are referred to as *mahajan* (merchant banker), *banya* [merchant moneylender), and *sahukar* [banker moneylender]. These phrases are parallel to the Qur'anic statement concerning those who devour (*ya'kiluna*) *riba*. The Persian derivative word *sood* literally means profit but in Urdu it is clearly related to the practices of the moneylenders. It is reasonable to assume that discussion on this subject in Pakistan is significantly influenced by the images and stereotypes associated with these phrases. However, these phrases may also support the view of those who believe that the focus of the Qur'anic injunction is on *riba* for consumer loans (Katouzian 1981: 102).

Looking at the question as a rural-urban issue, the small and traditional businessmen in cities would be inclined to support elimination of interest as they did during the period of General Ziaul Haq's Islamicization of the economy, hoping for a reprieve from their debt. It is also feasible that the entrepreneurs in big business would join the anti-*riba* lobby if they conduct their profit-making activity using traditional rather modern accounting techniques. It would be a bonus for big business when not only their profligate borrowings are written off but the cost of the loan is wiped out as well. In the rural sector, the feudal elements would welcome any opportunity to forgo the burden of interest. It seems that the poor are not affected by the financial structure of the country. Either they live and die in debt, or if they are lucky they may rely on mutual self-help or a 'committee' system in which a pool of funds is created to help members with major expenditures and loans are paid off through regular subscriptions. The data are lacking in this regard but anecdotal evidence seems to support this contention.

When the general socio-economic conditions are brought into play the question of *riba* assumes a broader meaning. It then becomes an unjustified increase in capital, whether in loan or 'sales' for which no equal compensation is given (Ziaul Haque 1985: 17). The essence of *riba* then is that the advanced sum of value, money or commodity, must not only be returned in original to the lender but it must also increase in value and be returned with a surplus (*fazl*) the rate of which varies with the state of the actual economic conditions (p. 17). Dr Haque takes issue with Fazlur Rahman for the latter's attempt to emphasize only the continuous redoubling aspect of *riba* (p. 50). Referring to Ibn Arabi and other juristic sources, he concludes that *riba* must be taken in a broad sense and it is intrinsic to both loans and sales. *Riba al-fazl* is thus a derivative and a corollary of *riba al-nasi'a*, because money and commodities are mutually exchangeable (p. 57). The tension is between *riba* and *bay'*, the former being the unearned income and the latter resulting from genuine exchange activity. Therefore *riba al-fazl* is not just an 'adjunct' of *al-riba* as Maudoodi asserted.

When *riba* is defined in a broader sense, it gives significance to the distribution of means of production in an economy. The earnings of property-owners, for example, without their contributing any productive activity becomes morally unjustified. This fact becomes obfuscated when emphasis is only on *riba al nasi'a*. 'The modern interpretation of *riba* by liberal modernists (as illegal usury), 'Islamic' economists, and orthodox ulama (as interest and usury), in reality reflects the struggle between the forces of semi-feudalism and industrial capitalism, between obscurantism and enlightenment (Ziaul Haque 1993: 942)

Riba and Reality

Debt and usury have been a matter of concern for religious and political leaders for a long time in the history of mankind. Solon's reform of the Athenian constitution, for example, included a cancellation of public and private debt. In the Roman Republic, interest was forbidden altogether, though the law could not be rigorously enforced. Later, a policy for a 'reasonable interest' was adopted. In the early Christian period, the taking of interest was banned. Charlemagne made usury a criminal offence. By the fifteenth century, the anti-usury position of the *Church* had reached its peak. The teachings of the *Church* emphasized that interest was a form of unearned income, a gain without labour, expense or risk on the part of the lender. But this principle was not applied consistently and other forms of unearned income such as rent from land, were permitted (Birnie 1952; Noonan 1957).

The Schoolmen further refined the issue. The concept of 'Just Price' was used to support the ban, though a loophole was created in its application when St. Thomas recognized that the credit price might be the normal price and that cash price might be based on a discounted value. Further, the concept of Roman Law was applied selectively to justify the position of the Church. A premium charged on *commodatum* (accomodation for the use of something which remains the property of the lessor) was justified, but not for *mutuum* (ownership is temporarily transferred, such as in the case of a loan). The lender was entitled only to what he had lent and no more. However, exceptions emerged, and a justification known as *damnum emergen* (a possible loss due to default) and *lucrum cessans* [opportunity for investment forgone were offered for interest (*interesse* = between)] on the loan. The latter explanation opened the door for linking interest with profits, though opportunities for alternative investment were not many during the period. It was a recognition of the causal power of money independent of labour. Another development—the triple contract—diluted the criterion of incidence of risk. On the eve of the Reformation, the Church condemned interest, but could not decide about the question of evasions.

Calvin perceived a close link between interest and rent as both being forms of unearned income. If one was justified, then, why not the other? Consequently, the use of interest starting with the Protestant countries gradually spread throughout Europe. Only the question about the 'reasonable' rate of interest was occasionally raised in public policy debate.

In Islamic jurisprudence, the focus has been on a specific dichotomy between *riba* and *bay'*. As mentioned above, the Qur'an does not offer a definition of *riba* because the practice was well known among the Arabs of the pre-Islamic period. What was the scope and nature of moneylending in Arabia? The answer to this question is based mostly on conjectures and deductive inferences from the traditions which seem to contradict each other. Also, how developed was the economy of Mecca? For Patricia Crone, Meccan trade was a local trade, in the sense that commodities traded were of Arabian origin and were for Arabian needs. It was not a trade generated by the commercial appetite of the surrounding empires (Crone 1987, Chap. 7). Mahmood Ibrahim takes a different approach and describes the organic connection between the sacred institutions in Mecca and the rise of commerce. The sources of accumulation of capital were *Ilaf* (commercial agreement) and *riba*, with *sadaqah* serving as a means of distribution of wealth. With the decline of tribal homogeneity and the rise of a differentiated structure, Mecca was ready for the message of the Prophet. Similarly, in Medina the social conditions were propitious to receive the Prophet's message of the unity of believers (Ibrahim 1980: 41ff).

If Crone's hypothesis is accepted, then Lammens' (and Maudoodi's) assertion that pre-Islamic Mecca was a thriving financial centre cannot be supported. (Father Lammen's place in this literature is considered quite weak even among the Western scholars of Islam.) And Ibrahim's analysis does not provide any evidence in this regard. The practice of *riba*, therefore must have been of the type normally associated with traditional societies. The distinction, then, between consumption and production loans becomes immaterial, though it may safely be assumed that in most cases the services of the moneylenders must have been used to meet the basic needs of the borrowers.

With the rise of commerce in the Muslim world during the medieval period the use of money increased in the economy. New methods to finance investment and trade were developed. Cash payments were too restrictive and credit to meet the needs of business was required. The price of credit transaction was necessarily higher than the cash transactions. Whether it was a discount on cash or premium on deferred transaction, interest was embedded in the practice (Udovitch 1975). Therefore, in order to avoid a formal resemblance with *riba*, juristic law, especially in the Hanafi tradition, was developed to accommodate the needs of business. The resolution to the conflict between legal niceties and economic necessities was based on two concepts: *istihsan* (juristic preference) and *hiyal* (legal devices). When it was noticed, for example, that *modaraba* was not suitable for transactions relating to physical capital, the rules of *ijarah* (lease) were developed so that the owner of machinery and other property could be paid a fee in lieu of its use by the entrepreneur. Further when limits of cash transactions started to affect the expanding economic activity, the seemingly commercial instruments were interjected in credit arrangements: a contract for deferred payment for goods [*bay' muajjal*] or an advance payment for future delivery [*bay' salam*]. These formal contracts were in fact subterfuges in order to legitimize the use of credit (Saleh 1986, especially p. 71ff). As Rodinson says, Muslim society provided itself with ideological precepts that conflicted with its practice, and had to find a solution to the problem (Rodinson 1974: 45–6).

It was with the advent of modern commercial banking and finance in the West that Muslim society faced a direct challenge to the question of *riba*. In the Ottoman Empire, there was a slow and gradual recognition of commercial interest. With the development of banking in the Empire, the use of commercial interest spread quickly. However, emphasis was on low rate of interest, which was considered compatible with the injunctions of Islam (Cagatay 1966). Going back further in Muslim history, one would find that the political regimes showed sensitivity to the realities of their economies. During the Abbasid period, especially in the 4th century of Hijra, there was a significant growth in financial institutions (*jahabizah* and *Sarraf*) practising modernistic banking techniques, including exchange of currencies, deposits, loans, and cashing of cheques (Islam 1989).

The above subterfuges, however, became part of the Islamic monetary reform introduced in Pakistan in 1988. The juristic innovations of Ottoman period were completely ignored. The crux of the reform is profit-and-loss (PLS) principle which the ulama and the Islamic economists endorse as the only method of financing replacing interest. It is the basis of Islamic banking of other business organizations such as *musharaka* (partnership) and *modaraba* (command a financing or trust financing) (Ahmed et al. 1987).

If the purpose is to remove any semblance with interest in regard to the income received by the owners of capital, then only the realized profits will be distributed upon termination of a business project, in order to make sure that the link between profits (or losses) and the enterprise is direct and identifiable. In the Hanafi tradition, the partnership may be of specific type or for general business. According to the Maliki school, the partnership is formed to conduct business in a single commodity or transaction. The rules set by the classical Islamic jurists, when interpreted in a literal sense, will require that the entrepreneurial activity is run on a modest scale and is of short duration. Only in such a situation could the investors wait for their share of profits without suffering undue hardship (Hardie and Rabooy 1991).

The modern enterprise has become extremely complex and time-consuming, however, owing to the ever-changing technology. The financing of this kind of enterprise would necessarily require periodic payments to the investors corresponding to the expected rates of return on a given portfolio of investments. In this process, the principle of averages would have to be used. Consequently, the juristic criterion of direct link between risk and dividends would disappear. Nevertheless, partnership and trust financing have an important role to play in the economic development of the country. Can PLS type of equity financing replace interest-based economic activity? Under certain conditions PLS financing may be more efficient than interest-based financing as suggested in a recent article (Presley and Sessions). The point, however, is whether the entire economy can be transformed into this mode with a view to eliminating any role for interest as it is used in modern times. Also, can PLS be established so that the share received by each individual partner is directly related to the risk taken by him. This question is further discussed in Chapter 4 below. No satisfactory answer has been provided by the Islamic economists in this regard. As Yaqub Shah pointed out, an average owner of capital would prefer security of lower discounted income as against expectation for a larger reward through profit-sharing, and there was nothing un-Islamic about it. Similarly, productive debt plays a role in business activity as its cost is known and can be calculated. These factors seem to persist in the economy behind the facade of PLS. There is, therefore, no 'pure' PLS system in existence, as both the security-oriented small investor as well as the entrepreneur in search of a judicious mix of equity and debt have to be accommodated through a variety of subterfuges.

Nawab Haider Naqvi takes a somewhat middle position on *riba* in view of practical problems which arise with reference to the Islamic modes of financing. For him '[a]bolishing *riba*, if interpreted as interest in the modern sense of the term, is really about replacing *riba* by a set of policy instruments which perform the same functions presumably more efficiently and equitably' (Naqvi 1994: 117). Towards this objective, PLS will have to be properly regulated to recognize the place for a risk-averse owner of funds (p. 131), and saving will have to be appropriately indexed to reflect inflation and the rate of growth of the economy.

The fundamental question remains, however. If *riba* is forbidden because there is no direct link invloved in it between risk incurred and profits received, as claimed by the ulama and the Islamic economists, then this criterion gets completely diluted in the complex network of 'evasive' financial instruments, and the debate is reduced to semantics.

NOTES

1. This chapter is based on the author's article entitled 'Pakistan and the Question of Riba', published in *Middle Eastern Studies*, 30:1, January 1994.
2. *See*, for example, Chapra (1985), Khan (1985), Mannan (1986), Siddiqi (1970 and 1981), Ahmed et al. (1987).

CHAPTER 4

Islamicizing the Banks

The reconstruction of the financial structure of a Muslim
country would require, first, the establishment of a national
commission to define the goals of economic policy in the
context of domestic and international developments and
then, secondly, to have an open and a thorough discussion
of the areas of possible reform in the system. When the
issue of the constitution was finally settled in 1973, there
was an opportunity to review the national economic policy
and the place of the financial system in it. Mr Z.A. Bhutto,
instead found it politically expedient to nationalize the
banks. Under General Ziaul Haq, the Islamicization of
banks and some related financial institutions was
implemented in the same manner. The Council of Islamic
Ideology received presidential order on 29 September 1979
to prepare a blueprint for interest-free economic system. A
panel of economists and bankers was appointed in
November of that year which submitted its recommendations to the Council in February 1980. The Council
considered these recommendations and then prepared its
final report in June 1980. Thus, the complex issue of
overhauling the economic system was settled in less than
one year.

It was at best a disingenuous effort, because the gap
between the views of the ulama and those of the financiers
was wider than it was admitted by either side and the views
of the ulama prevailed at the Council. The reform was
imposed on the reluctant financiers and they adjusted to it
in a manner that left the banks more powerful under the

so-called interest-free system than they were in the interest-based regime, essentially practising traditional banking under a new name. Recently, a manifesto was issued by the International Institute of Islamic Economics of the Islamic University at Islamabad asking the government to establish the Islamic financial system without further delay. It notes that the Council made compromises in its recommendations which were contrary to the sharia and that the true system should be in complete conformity with the injunctions of Islam, as interpreted by the Institute. The proposal made by the Institute indicates that very little progress has been made in the Islamic economic thought in the last twenty years.

The purpose of this chapter is to give a brief summary of the banking reforms, to examine the feasibility of the new instruments of financing which have been deemed acceptable to the ulama, and to extend the conclusions of Chapter 3 concerning the question of *riba* versus *bay'* and its relevance in modern times.

The New Legal Framework for Islamic Banking

Several ordinances were proclaimed on the authority of General Ziaul Haq to change the financial structure of the country. The salient features of these ordinances are summarized in Appendix I to this chapter. The purpose of these ordinances was to bring about a drastic shift in the legal traditions of the country. They are, however, the product of hasty drafting, insulated from the critical scrutiny of parliamentary or public debate. Also, they have created a peculiar patchwork of amendments, often out of tune, and sometimes in conflict, with the main substance of the old acts. The Companies Ordinance, 1984, for example, has turned out to be a fascinating interest-based old document with glimpses of interest-free banking. It was in the context of this kind of ordinances that Islamic banking was introduced in 1980, starting with optional profit-and-loss sharing (PLS) bank deposits replacing interest, and rent-sharing replacing mortgage rates charged by the House Building Finance Corporation. In June 1984, the State Bank of Pakistan issued a directive defining what is referred to as the 'twelve modes of Islamic banking' which were to be the sole basis of financial activities of the banks from July 1985. These modes of financing may be described as follows (State Bank of Pakistan 1984: xvi–xx):

1. Financing by lending: two kinds of loans are permitted in this category. The first carries a service charge not exceeding the *proportionate* cost of the operation but excluding the cost of funds as well as a provision for bad and doubtful debts [Italics provided]. This service charge appears to be an approximate substitute for the market interest rate and is subject to a maximum limit as determined by the State Bank of Pakistan. The second type of loan is interest-free, given on compassionate grounds, *qarze-e-hasna*, and it is due when the borrower is able to meet his obligation.

2. Trade-related financing: there are six methods recommended in this category which include the sale and purchase of goods and trade bills at appropriate mark-up or mark-down in prices on a deferred payment basis, lending by means of buy-back agreement in which the bank acquires the title of goods or securities at an agreed price and the borrower accepts to purchase the same goods or securities at a higher price at the end of the specified period, as well as leasing and hire-purchase financing of a variety of consumer and producer goods. These arrangements are similar to the system of contract devised in the medieval period of Islam as referred to in Chapter 3 above.

3. Investment type financing: four methods of financing are included in this category: i) *musharaka* (partnership) on PLS basis; ii) equity participation and purchase of shares; iii) purchase of participation term certificates (PTC) and *modaraba* certificates (a system in which the skill of

management is combined with finances provided by subscribers); and iv) rent-sharing such as in housebuilding.

The combined effect of the above ordinances and State Bank directives is a mixed package in which commercial banks are permitted to engage in equity financing and commercial loan activities. It seems, however, that in both cases, especially with regard to the latter, the practical effect is to redefine the role of interest in the Islamic modes. Consequently, the banks seem to have met the new challenge by resorting mainly to mark-up and mark-down in their lending operations. What are the ethical implications of lending by acquiring title of goods not already in possession of the lender is a serious question. In the various schools of Islamic jurisprudence the only problem that has received serious attention is concerning *khiyar al-ru'ya* (the purchaser having the option to reject the object of sale after inspection) (Saleh 1986: 67). This option is not available in Pakistan (Shahrukh Rafi Khan 1987: 142). In any case, the borrower is assumed to have the knowledge about the subject of sale, the bank only acquires the title to make the credit arrangement legitimate in law. The main difference, then, between a traditional bank loan and the Islamic bank loan is the extra paper work involved in determining the appropriate collateral for the loan. Credit is thus fully entrenched in the new banking system of Pakistan. For the repayment of loan on schedule, the mark-up is reduced by a bonus. In case of default the traditional banking charges such as compound interest effect have been substituted with more serious penalties under the provisions of the Banking Tribunal Ordinance which provide for a prompt and ruthless method of recovery of loans (Patel 1986: 72). Originally, the courts established under this Ordinance were expected to settle cases within thirty days, and in the event of a delay in clearing the disputes, a full mark-up was calculated to cover the cost of the maximum period involved, thus giving the bank a considerable advantage over the borrower (Gieraths

1990:184). A recent change in the system of recovery of loans is expected to accelerate the pace of clearing the dues. An increase in the number of courts would make it possible to resolve the claims, without delay, with thirty days as a maximum limit. It is reported that the amount involved in these cases is about Rs 120 billion (*Dawn*, August 28, 1997)

The Impact on the Financial Structure

The financial structure of Pakistan consists of a reasonably developed non-securities market, the central bank, the commercial banks including foreign-owned banks, and the developing stock exchanges in Karachi and Lahore. In addition, there are several federal and provincial cooperative banks, specialized financial institutions, and a few insurance companies. Savings in Pakistan are mostly channelled through bank deposits, and national savings schemes. The main source of voluntary savings are households including the fluctuating foreign remittances from Pakistanis abroad. While banks have moved to the so-called modes of Islamic financing, the national savings schemes are still based on interest, now called 'profit', and so are the public bonds and securities.

Prior to the introduction of Islamic banking, therefore, there was a modest process of financial deepening taking place, with the then nationalized commercial banks, cooperative banks, and specialized corporations representing the growth of financial intermediation. The role of government, apart from its regulation of the financial market, was visible through its national debt and fiscal policy. The bank rate was set at 10 per cent during 1985, indicating no change since 1977. Parallel to the bank rate, conventional advances by commercial banks were permitted at a ceiling of 14 per cent per annum. Other rates for long term loans ranged between 9 per cent and 14 per cent per annum. These were all nominal rates and what the effect of inflation was on real rates is difficult to say. Currency in circulation as a ratio of GNP was stable during this period. Also, the liquidity ratio of banks remained above the prescribed minimum. (State Bank of Pakistan, 1985b). The State Bank of Pakistan played an important role as a final monetary authority in the country. It pursued a policy of selective credit controls for particular purposes. Traditionally, commercial banks concentrated on short-term financing but they also maintained lines of credit for selected clients to allow them to use short-term funds for medium-term objectives (Meenai 1966 & 1984). It was a regulated structure, somewhat 'repressed', according to the McKinnon-Shaw criteria (McKinnon 1973; Shaw 1973); Shaw, in his discussion, uses Pakistan strategy as an example of financial repression (Shaw 1973: 108–112). (Financial repression is generally identified to occur when there is a weak incentive to save and to invest in an economy. With interest rate at 10 per cent, for example, the expected reward on a deposit would be neutralized if inflation was taking place at the same rate. There is of course a parellel argument according to which low savings may be the result of an undeveloped national financial structure) (*see* Ashfaque H. Khan 1988).

The House Building Finance Corporation (HBFC) shifted to the unregulated profit and loss system, when the first phase of Islamic banking was introduced. The HBFC, in its calculation of the new formula for rent-sharing arrived at the same rate structure that was used for conventional mortgages prior to the introduction of PLS (Salamat Ali 1981a). The commercial banks started to use mark-up for all their short term business from July 1985 when the complete change-over in the system was implemented. The price of goods at which loans could be granted was determined on the basis of paisas per thousand daily products with a minimum and a maximum established by the Pakistan Banking Council, originally in the range of 10 to 19 per cent and later revised to 12–16 per cent (State Bank of Pakistan, 1985a). (The 'product' may be taken, broadly speaking, as synonymous with productive activity. When funds are borrowed, these funds are expected to be in use on a daily basis while in possession of the borrower. The mark-up in paisas per 1000 daily products at 10 paisas per annum would amount to a 1 percent interest rate, or mark-up, as the banks prefer to call it). What criteria were used to determine the range of mark-up prices is not clear, but there is a close resemblance to the weighted average of the old rate structure used by banks for commercial advances.

In addition to their short-term lending on the basis of PLS, the banks also got involved in long-term investment through National Development Finance Corporation, the Bankers' Equity, and other approved enterprises. Their credit activities continued to be strictly controlled and their allocation among various loan categories such as private and public enterprises was fixed by the State Bank. The new instruments of financing investments on PLS basis became Participating Term Certificate (PTC) and Term Financing Certificate (TFC), authorized under the Companies Ordinance, 1980. The former is fully transferable and the latter is a kind of debenture sold at a premium as arranged between the financial institution and the borrower.

There is no official market rate of interest under the new system, as it is formally an interest-free system. The producers face two kinds of cost considerations: mark-up and the PLS. In the case of the mark-up, the sale price of the subject involved is calculated on the basis of 'daily products' as mentioned above. If, for example, the purchase price of goods is fixed by the bank at $100 for a deferred sale at $105 at the end of 365 days, then it is equivalent to interest rate of 5 per cent per annum. There are differences between the mark-up and interest which should be noted, however. Lending under mark-up is necessarily commodity-specific, but lending with interest need not have any such constraint. Also, the mark-up is tied to the expected price of the goods involved in the transaction. It is related not only to the credit-worthiness of the borrower, but also to the nature of his business. It would require higher administrative cost for its operation than interest because of a double moral hazard created by the unavoidable link between the loan and the goal of the transaction. (Moral hazard occurs when two parties to a contract have unequal access to information. The possibility that a depositor's funds with a financial institution may be used to help enterprises of dubious credit-worthiness is an example of moral hazard.) For all these reasons, mark-up would tend to promote market segmentation, a tendency that may occur under interest-based regime but would probably not be as strong as in the mark-up mode. [Segmentation may involve a focus on a single transaction, with no comparative information about alternatives.] The price of loan in this mode would most likely increase as compared to the competitive interest market.

From mark-up to PLS is a shift from debt to equity. How the decision-making of the producer is affected by PLS may be discussed with reference to *musharaka* and *modaraba* financing. The former is a temporary partnership between one or more owners of capital and entrepreneurs for a specific period of time. It is designed to provide working capital needs of a company. The client is responsible for the business and the owner of capital, usually a bank, would examine the feasibility of the project and supervise its operation. Profits are shared as agreed and the distribution of profits may not correspond to the capital contributions of the respective parties. However, losses must be shared in proportion to the respective investment shares (Habib Bank 1986: 16).

Modaraba financing is considered the ultimate goal of interest-free economy. A *modaraba* company is an entity that combines entrepreneurial skill with subscribed capital of shareholders. During the medieval period of Islam, *modaraba* represented a profit-sharing arrangement in commercial enterprises. It has been modified to fit in with the modern banking operation. The criterion of PLS demands that there be no element of debt in this mode of financing. However, debt-equity mix is considered to be a useful device of financial planning by corporations in industrial countries. The Modigliani-Miller theorem casts doubts about its importance. The theorem draws on the data relating to the interest-based industrial economies where, according to the authors, a leverage of financing within a range would have no effect on the cost of financing for a corporation (Modigliani and Miller 1958). [I have already discussed the question of debt-equity ratio with reference to Syed Yaqub Shah. My purpose in referring to this theorem is to show that in neoclassical economics this issue has received some attention. In an interest-free economy the bonds would disappear, being an important element of debt financing, and total financing in a *Modaraba* would be based on PLS, a kind of equity. In the world of Modigliani-Miller, bonds may disappear, without affecting the leverage of financing, albeit within a range, but various kinds of shares would continue to play their role, such as preferred shares establishing a commitment for a certain rate of return. Also, when annual dividends are paid in the interest-based economies, there is no necessary link between these dividends and the corresponding risk incurred by a shareholder.]

The theorem is based on highly restrictive assumptions, limiting its general applicability, and it may be especially difficult to extend it to the extreme situation of interest-free financing. In any case, the principle of debt-equity mix could be easily followed in the PLS mode by a judicious combination of investment funds, the lease and the mark-up loans. Also, the question is not, as I said in Chapter 3 above, whether equity financing is more flexible and efficient than debt-equity financing as it is claimed by some advocates of PLS system (e.g., W.M. Khan 1985, M.S.Khan 1986). It is whether *modaraba* type financing would dispense with interest as we know it in modern times.

The Islamic economists often point out that there is no consensus about the theory of interest among the neoclassical economists. What determines interest rate and which theory best explains the phenomenon is not the real issue. There is the well-known Keynesian approach to interest rate, and there are the nonmonetary theories which make an attempt to explain the phenomenon. The relation between the two approaches is quite complex and it need not be discussed here. A focus on the nonmonetary variables seems appropriate for our discussion, however, because the Islamic economists recognize the rate of return as a reward only when capital is combined with enterprise, but deny the usefulness of interest in the economy. The nonmonetary focus includes all the relevant explanations which can be employed to discuss the 'necessity' of interest. There is the position taken by the classical economists, on the one hand, which ignored the distinction between capital and enterprise. In the neoclassical tradition this distinction is emphasized and is discussed with various dimensions added by Bohm-Bawerk, Fisher, Schumpeter, Knight, and Ramsey (Conard 1963).

I propose to offer a brief examination of the question in the remaining part of this section. The discussion may be somewhat terse for the non-economist. There is an attempt made in Appendix II to this chapter to explain the main points in a simpler language.

Irving Fisher provides a succinct treatment of how and why interest is determined (Conard). Any observed market interest consists of the following: $r_1 = r + r' + r''_1$, where 'r' may be identified as Fisher's 'appreciation' factor, 'r''_1' as a particular risk premium including equity without any collateral, and 'r' as the 'pure' interest on a security '$_1$'. In this manner, the security is said to represent the rate of return to the physical capital, and the market interest disseminates information about alternative investment opportunities. The question raised by the advocates of interest-free economy is a simple one: is it possible to allocate resources without first having some information about the supply and demand for loanable funds in the market, i.e. the market interest rate. If a firm, for example, is in the business of renting machines to other firms, how would it calculate the opportunity cost of funds tied up in the machine in an interest-free economy? Also, in discussions of interest-free economy, profit and rate of return are used interchangeably, but profit is not defined. It is then claimed that under PLS, the (expected) profit would play the same role that interest plays in allocating resources to the best use. It seems then that the expected profit, or the periodic payments on the basis of the expected rate of return becomes a proxy for interest in the PLS system. It is a kind of non-discounting approach to investment decisions.

There are many non-discounting methods used by firms in industrial economies. These include payback method, peak period method, and the average profit of accounting return method which are explained in detail in the relevant literature (Hawkins and Pearce 1971; Bromwich 1976). However, it is one thing to use non-discounting methods in an interest-based system where interest plays its ultimate role in determining alternative use of funds, and quite another to try to build the whole economy on the basis of non-discounting criteria. It is possible that the importance of this distinction will become gradually apparent as the tradition of project evaluation is more fully developed in the country. The basic significance of the criterion of discounted value is to show that the future value of a present sum is greater than its present value, so the present worth of a sum due later on is less than its future value. For example, $100 to be received four years from now has a discounted value of $88.50 at 3 per cent compounded annually. Similarly, if an individual invests $100 instead of using it on current consumption, then he would expect to be paid the principal and an additional sum in the future which would constitute the future value of the present sum. Both the accountant and the economist are interested in this phenomenon. The economist tries to explain it and, in so doing, he invokes any or all the familiar variables used in the nonmonetary theories of interest, such as Bohm-Bawerk's round-about method of production and time preference, or scarcity of capital in the Knight-Ramsey framework. In other words, capital theory attempts to elucidate the causes and consequences of acts of saving and investment, and towards this objective it also emphasizes the microeconomics of pricing, involving rentals, interest rates and present value (Solow 1963).

It should be noted, however, that the connection between interest and discount is quite complex (Baumol 1977). The concept of interest is broader and it covers all kinds of costs which accrue automatically with the passage of time, and it must be carefully adjusted to accomodate changing price level in the economy. Discount rate, on the other hand, represents opportunity cost of obtaining funds later rather than now. So long as interest rate market exists, the relation between the two concepts can be worked out. In the interest-free economy it is not possible to bridge the information gap unless the structure of the economy is changed where almost the entire producer goods sector is socialized, where social discount rate becomes a proxy for the market discount rate.

The problem facing the Islamic economists would not disappear insofar as the market mechanism is permitted in the Islamic economy. It does not of course mean that this problem gets resolved in a non-market system; it only reappears in various subterfuges which are employed to allocate funds to various uses. In their holdings of investment portfolios, individuals are bound to compare present values of assets in order to make rational choices. Discounting in this sense is a behavioural reality. Of course, time preference is not as universal as Bohm-Bawerk assumed. Nor is it as unimportant as claimed by the Islamic economists. People of course do not ignore their future, in subjective terms, and they would try to put away part of their present income for various reasons, including precautionary motives. The possibility for a neutral time preference, nevertheless, is very small as long as people on the whole would like to plan streams of income through saving and borrowing, and as long as the economic growth is fostered by productivity changes or through net increase in stock of capital. It seems, therefore, that in an interest-free framework, the market would continue to search for the pure interest rate at a suboptimal level of performance. The other elements of the market interest would probably be shifted into accounting profits as risk variables or skill and management factors, especially with reference to large projects and big enterprises. If there were no time preference in an Islamic economy, as the advocates of interest-free system claim, then it would be unnecessary to collect information about the 'expected' rates of return from investments and to offer premiums on term certificates.

The Scope of Commercial Banking

In Chapter 3, it was emphasized that the classical jurists of Islam evolved their ideas concerning the dichotomy of *riba* versus *bay'* by focusing on the principle of risk-taking. Given the fact that commercial activity can cover a wide range of transactions and it would require credit facilities to provide working finance for these transactions, various *hiyal* methods were accepted as legitimate as long as the risk factor in a given commercial activity was clearly identified. It was a challenge to keep the *hiyal* from becoming identified with interest under cover of different nomenclatures.

In the modern industrial economy, with the institution of commercial banking incorporating all the advanced techniques of financing, the grafting of the *hiyal* in their operations is bound to create a situation in which the subterfuges would be easily absorbed into the existing system of finance, and they would serve to maintain the stability of the system. The fundamental principle of modern banking is the pooling of funds for financing diverse activities, and to keep it solvent by comparing and keeping in line the average costs and benefits from these activities over a period of time. This principle is incompatible with the criterion of risk-taking as defined in the classical Islamic jurisprudence.

The report of the Council of Islamic Ideology (Ziauddin et al. 1982) which formed the basis of the banking reform recommended *bay' muajjal* as a mode of short-term-financing but hedged it with various reservations. It assumed that this method would be used only sparingly by the banking system (paragraphs 1.16 and 1.17). In fact it has emerged as the main form of financial arrangement against 'collateral' of goods subject to mark-up by the banks in the country. Another example which shows that the Council was confused about the issue concerns the operations of the banks under PLS. The illustration given in the report (paragraphs 2.31 and 2.32) relies on the distribution of average profits and losses among various depositors on the basis of weighted daily products of the amounts kept in the deposit liabilities of the banks. An observation recently made with regard to the Egyptian banking reform is very apt for Pakistan as well: 'From a religious viewpoint, the fact that the returns to the depositors are not related to a specific project but are rather tied to a time dimension implies that this system is similar to that based on interest' (Kazarian 1993: 87). In the averages the gains and losses become diluted. When it is the question of receiving a share in average profits, the recipients would gladly accept the payment. However, if the losses should occur, the 'enlightened' self-interest of those who believe that they might be paying for other peoples' mistakes would seriously threaten the system. There are indications that the evil effects of the borrower's irresponsible, even dishonest, behaviour are being suffered by the innocent depositors in the banking system of the country (Naqvi 1994: 143).

The advocates of interest-free banking emphasize that in the Islamic system the rate of return to deposits would increase and savings would be encouraged. This is supposed to result both from efficiency of the PLS system as against the fixed return from interest, as well as the *zakat* on 'idle' assets. The data do not seem to support this contention. The rate of return on savings accounts has shown a *secular* decline during 1981–6 (Gierath 1990: 191–3), and the trend seems to have continued beyond 1986 to 1991 according to the latest survey (Naqvi 1994: 141–3). It seems that the savers are more risk-averse than assumed by the Islamic economists. Also, would the imposition of *zakat* spur people to transfer their savings into investment? No study has been done to examine this question; only the a priori assumptions dominate the literature on this subject.

The Role of the *Modaraba*

The long term investment, according to interest-free financing, must be based on profit- and loss-sharing. The Shariat Court judgement of 1991 which declared all laws based on interest as repugnant to Islam also emphasized that *modaraba* was the most acceptable form of investment (Key Law Reports 1992: 168–71).

As discussed in Chapter 3 above, payment of interest on money is forbidden according to the traditional ulama, because it is fixed and pre-determined. It is unjust because the lender manages to have his principal and an additional sum returned to him at the end of a specified period without sharing the risk of enterprise. Bohm-Bawerk was perhaps re-echoing the same sort of feeling when he admitted that 'interest accrues to the capitalist even when he has not moved a finger in its making' (Bohm-Bawerk 1890). He recognized, however, that there was a plausible explanation for interest in the economy as mentioned above. The PLS criterion requires that the capitalist be rewarded only from the realized profits. It is, however, not possible to assume that realized profits necessarily represent a fair reward. Frank Knight reminds us that there is little ethical basis for presuming that a man's just deserts are at all closely correlated with the value that emerges from his products. This holds true even under conditions of pure competition, and more so in the real world where value can be inflated by contrived scarcity (Conard 1963: 102). And when it is a question of average profits from a group of projects, the criterion of interest-free returns to the so-called risk-taking investors becomes highly questionable from the point of view of *riba*, as defined by the traditional ulama.

What is the component of 'excess' in profits, whether earned from *modaraba* or sale of mutton, can be further linked with the Marxian theory of exploitation, or to a broader Islamic concept of *riba al-fazl*. In fact, the unearned income received from *riba al-nasi'a* may not compare in magnitude with the rentier element in *riba al-fazl*. The emphasis on the former and the concomitant indifference towards the latter, however, superbly suits the economic interests of the elite in the country.

The classical jurists rationalized the economic relationship prevailing in the traditional agricultural-commercial society in the form of *modaraba* (Ziaul Haque 1985: 220). In its modified form, it would be a useful organizational device in promoting industrial development of the country. Its role in establishing the principle of PLS, however, is highly doubtful. During the last ten years, there has been a phenomenal growth in *modaraba* companies. They can be classified as specific or multi-purpose, for specific period or without time limit. Most of these companies are mainly in leasing business, with Grindlays dominating the sector. In addition, there are companies which exclusively specialize in leasing business. The leased assets are mostly in plants and machinery for textile, steel, and services sectors (Pakistan and Gulf Economist 1993 28). It may be said that the rapid growth of modarabas was due to the need for medium and small scale investment which was not being filled by the existing system. It is, therefore, possible to argue that this growth may have already reached its plateau and further expansion of these companies will depend on a variety of factors including the general growth of the economy.

The leasing companies depend on funds raised through share capital and lines of credit from banks or international organizations. The *modaraba* companies raise their capital through Participating Term Certificates (PTCs), and in order to qualify for tax exemptions, they must distribute 90 per cent of their profits after deducting 10 per cent for their professional fees. These companies, in principle, are established to replace interest-based system by risk-taking through PLS. In fact, their operations and functions are all designed to minimize risk. First, the leasing business is, as mentioned earlier, as secure as a fixed loan with interest. Secondly, the purchase price of PTCs incorporates the opportunity cost of capital, implicitly validating the role of interest (Shahrukh Rafi Khan 1987: 143–4). Also, the concept of fixed rate of return is built into the PTCs, so that if the profit shares exceed a certain limit, the excess is credited to a special reserve fund which, if necessary may be used to cover any possible losses (Khan: 144). Although, the loss absorption is implicit in the PTCs, the question still remains whether it is morally justified to hold the lender responsible for the loss (Naqvi 1994: 125–6). This is a hangover from the medieval modaraba which is clearly out of tune with modern times. This is especially the case when the *modaraba* provisions do not limit the number of entrepreneurs following the initial investment. If among any four companies, the last one earns a profit, all four are allowed to retain their respective shares. In case of loss, the initial certificate holder must bear the whole burden (Gieraths 1990: 188).

The *modaraba* contract is likely to create a moral hazard like that in the mark-up system, but in a different context. The share of the entrepreneur is fixed in advance at the time when he receives the investment fund. The investor, however, cannot effectively monitor the administration of the enterprise once the contract is signed (Kazarian: 99).

Conclusion

The reform of banks was an important area of Islamicization of General Ziaul Haq. The bankers wanted to proceed with caution. The Council of Islamic Ideology under the chairmanship of Dr Tanzilur Rahman was anxious for an immediate programme to eliminate interest from the economy, a programme which was endorsed later in 1991 by the Shariat Court with him as the chief justice of the court. The final report of the Council departed from the recommendations of the bankers in several important respects and it has been discussed elsewhere in the relevant literature (*see*, Gieraths 1980 for example).

It was also the period in which Islamic economics emerged, claiming to be a separate discipline. The main thrust of the literature under this title was that *riba* must be eliminated and that by definition it included modern interest. They built models to show that PLS was more efficient than interest-based financing. The implicit argument was that a modified form of equity financing would fulfil the juristic criteria concerning *riba*. There was a serious flaw in their argument and it was owing to the fact that the ulama on whose views they had based their conclusions had no training in economics and they themselves made no effort to seriously examine the relevant literature in the Islamic jurisprudence.

There were some exceptions concerning the role of PLS in the economy. It was argued, for example, that the PLS side by side the traditional banking system would be superior to a system in which PLS was the only mode of financing available to the entrepreneurs (Shahrukh Rafi Khan 1987). Of course, this mix of two distinct modes could create an adverse selection problem in which poor-risk potential borrowers rejected by the traditional banks may shift to the PLS (Cobham 1992: 244). A group of economists, however, argued that the pace of the Islamic reform should be made conditional upon the reform of the entire political economy of the country (Naqvi et al. 1980). One would never know how that fundamental change in the society would have been brought about. For General Ziaul Haq, Islamicization was a political necessity, in order to establish legitimacy of his rule. The politicians who have led the country since his death have not had the courage to confront the Islamic lobby and some of them found an opportunity for their survival in coveting support of this group. The financial structure of the country somehow continues to fulfil its role by resorting to subterfuges. The so-called Islamicization seems to promote deception as a way of doing business, weakening the element of honesty in the culture of the society.

Appendix I

Legal Framework for Islamic Banking

1. *Modaraba* Companies *Modaraba* (Floatation & Control) Ordinance, 1980. It provides for subscription to a company in which skill of management is combined with finances by subscribers. Profits are distributed among shareholders according to prior agreement and the entrepreneur is also entitled to a fee as a fixed percentage of net profits (Mansoor Book House, n.d.).

2. Amendments to the banking laws relevant for our discussion were made as follows: State Bank of Pakistan (Second Amendment) Ordinance, 1980; Banks (Nationalization-Amendment) Ordinance, 1980; and Banking Companies (Recovery of Loans) Amendment, 1980 (Habib Bank Ltd., 1986).

3. Companies Ordinance, 1980. It was aimed at amending 1972 act concerning the issue of managing agencies and election of directors (Mansoor Book House).

4. Banking and Finance Services (Amendment of Law) Ordinance, 1980. It was introduced to amend various statutes and to establish a legal framework for the Islamic banking system.

5. Banking Tribunal Ordinance, 1984. It is based on the assumption that banks under the new system are more vulnerable to defaults, and in order to strengthen their position and as mentioned in the chapter, the Ordinance provides for a prompt and 'ruthless method of recovery of loans' (Patel 1986: 72).

6. Companies Ordinance, 1984. It was introduced to accommodate new intruments of investment such as Participation Term Certificate (PTC) and *musharaka* cerificates. Capital raised through these certificates was to become part of the 'redeemable capital', a new concept introduced in the Ordinance to facilitate Profit-and-Loss Sharing (PLS) (Lahore Law Times Publications, n.d.).

Appendix II

In the classical tradition, broadly speaking, interest rate brings an economy into equilibrium in the long run. It is, therefore, linked with productive activity, i.e., the rate of return to the investment. The entrepreneur borrows funds up to a point where he derives sufficient income from his economic activity so that he may return the borrowed capital along with interest and have funds left over to pay for his other costs. In the neoclassical system, the emphasis is on market equilibrium and the questions are raised about how the rewards of the factors of production are determined. The literature, for example, is rich in theories addressing the issue of interest. Related to this phenomenon is the macroeconomic role of money in which the Quantity Theory underlines the direct link between money, price level, and interest rate. While the theories of interest were trying to explain the phenomenon, interest rate became a major tool of economic policy.

There is an important public policy assumption implicit in this approach: the economy will work in a broad framework of *laissez-faire* capitalism, through indirect control of money supply in relation to the ebb and flow of business activity. In recent years, it has been used to keep inflation at zero or near-zero level in the industrial countries at the cost of employment and full-time jobs. Would such a monetary policy work in a situation of a serious low-level economic cycle? There has not been a real test of this question since the Great Depression, when it failed.

Keynes' thinking was profoundly influenced by the events of the thirties, and the unflattering title of Depression economics was assigned to his theory by his critics. In recent years, Keynes has been blamed for persistently high levels of national debt and deficit which became the main feature of budgetary manipulation in the developed countries, even though these budgets were never devised according to the principles of Keynesian fiscal policy. The theory may yet turn out to be more resilient and more generally applicable. The mechanism which determines supply and demand of money and its effect on prices is quite complex, according to Keynes. Changes in money supply would affect interest, with upper and lower limits in this link—the problem of liquidity preference (holding on to funds in cash rather in a form of investment owing to uncertainties such as expected changes in interest rate). At the lower limit, for example, increase in money supply would have little impact on interest rate because people would hold money in that situation. Liquidity preference turns out to be a forceful concept to explain the limits of monetary policy. The desired investment expenditure, however, is sensitive to changes in interest rate, and in the Keynesian framework, there is no built-in tendency in the economy to create stability and employment. Interest rates, therefore, must be manipulated as part of the monetary policy to expand the economy. Hence the name of monetary theory of interest. The political implication of Keynesian theory is a proactive capitalist system in which government employs suitable tools to encourage investment and employment. Keynes does not contradict the long-run phenomenon and he muses about the possibility of a near-zero interest in an abundantly endowed economy.

The Fisher's equation underlines the factors which determine the market interest rate—the pure rate which is related to the long-run economic behaviour of the economy; and the other considerations such as risk of lending. Interest rate, then becomes the basis for discounting the future: what will be the value of $1 ten years from now, or how much is it worth today to become a $1 in ten years? Calculations are based on assumptions about how the economy would behave in the future. As the circumstances change, so do the calculations, and discount rate remains in a state of perennial adjustment, guided by the comparison between the estimated and the actual rate of return, as well as the expected and the realized profits.

There is also the phenomenon of inflation, corroding the purchasing power of money, and if it is not taken into account, the financial system in the economy becomes 'repressed'.

Interest is a price and it enters the cost of production like prices of other inputs including wages which are assumed as 'pre-determined' even by Islamic economists. The process between the beginning and end of production of a good goes through so many changes, anticipated as well as unanticipated that in the end profits earned may not represent the true reward for an according to entrepreneur, as emphasized by Frank Knight. This issue has never been clearly defined in Islamic economics.

CHAPTER 5

Property and Wealth

The principle of profit- and loss–sharing assumes that an individual has a right to own property. This right is circumscribed, of course, by the obligations imposed on the faithful to use their assets judiciously and in a righteous manner. According to the traditional view of Islamic jurisprudence, this would lead to the creation of an egalitarian system in the Islamic community. The question of ownership of land occupies an important place in the literature. Apart from the behavioural factor implicit in the Islamic view, there is a forceful institution of laws of inheritance which would not permit concentration of wealth in the society. My objective in this chapter is to focus on how the basic principles concerning property and wealth can be harmonized with the changing economic character of the society. My approach then will be to avoid discussion of details and to confine my analysis to the main points in the subject.

The Landlord and the Cultivator

A few years prior to the establishment of Pakistan, Maulana Hifzur Rahman, a senior fellow at Nadwa-tul-Musannifin, Delhi discussed this issue in his book in Urdu on the Islamic economic system (1939, rev. edn. and fourth reprint, 1951). He notes that the Qur'an gives a special place to agriculture as the main source for food and sustenance, and that the traditions of the Prophet underline the importance of agriculture in the life of the community (1951: 164ff). Quoting various jurists including Shah Waliullah, an eighteenth century Islamic reformer of Delhi, he concludes that the ultimate source of prosperity is agriculture. He suggests that the countries which excel in trade and industry would not be able to continue in their specialization without their links with the agricultural economies for their basic needs, the links which sometimes are imposed through imperial relationships.

Comparing Islam with capitalism and communism, he notes that individual ownership of land is permitted but is subject to clearly defined conditions. There are traditions of the Prophet which indicate that a person should possess only as much land as he can cultivate himself (p. 228ff.) There are other traditions, however, which impose no specific limits on ownership and suggest that the landlord may rent the excess land to a cultivator on the basis of sharecropping or cash payment. He notes that the share-cropping arrangement between the landlord and the tenant is a controversial issue and there is no clear consensus among the jurists about it. Historically, both systems seem to have been prevalent during the time of the Prophet and of the four Caliphs. The Prophet, however, seemed to have a clear preference for self-cultivation as against the renting of land which he thought fell below the standards of ethical behaviour and generosity— *akh'laq aur murrawat se nazil*. From this point of view, it can be argued that the state may forbid the system of landlordism in the interests of the community as a whole, and take away the excess holdings by means of proper compensation to the owner (p. 235).

Abul 'Ala Maudoodi published a book concerning the question under the title of *Mas'ala Milkiyyat-e-Zamin* in 1950 which was based on his commentaries published in his monthly journal *Tarjuman-ul Qur'an*, with revisions and additions included in the new book. The book has gone through several reprints, the latest being for 1994. It seems, however, that to prepare a section for his book on

Ma'ashi'at-e-Islam, edited by Khurshid Ahmad, he revised some of his arguments on the subject (1969). He emphasizes that the Qur'anic view on the matter is unmistakable, that it endorses private property as a legitimate form of personal possession. Concerning the scope and limit of ownership, he suggests that a person could own as much as he could legitimately manage. On the question of feudal estates and land grants, he argues that not all beneficiaries of the gift of land are alike and that a legitimate gift used with justice and fairness towards tenants is a proper mode of ownership (1969: 212).

Maudoodi examines the question of land reform in his *Milkiyyat-e-Zamin* (1950 and 1994), and suggests that any reform must satisfy four criteria: complete respect for private ownership, no nationalization, no attempt to impose equality of ownership, and no government restrictions on legitimate use of land (1994: 102–109). He is therefore against imposing legal means to protect an agricultural class by denying access to land to the non-agricultural classes. The land in rural areas should be open to any proper transactions for sale or purchase, like land in urban areas.

The landlord has the right, according to Maudoodi, to rent his excess land through a sharecropping arrangement or on the basis of profit- and loss-sharing (1950: 53; 1994: 79). In *Ma'ashi'at-e-Islam*, however, he defines the arrangement as profit-sharing with reference to the principle of *maza'rabat* (1969: 218). He notes that there are differences of views among the jurists concerning possession and use of excess land. And he suggests that apart from a few voices of dissent there is complete consensus in the juristic thought that ownership of land cannot be limited to self-cultivation. What should be the best method of rental arrangement is perhaps subject to a wider difference of opinion. In every juristic school of thought, one or the other method is endorsed (1994: 101).

The issue of *muzara'a* (sharecropping, metayage) in the early history of Islam is an important phenomenon. In his analysis of this issue, Dr Ziaul Haque (1977) presents a thorough examination of the views of the classical jurists in the context of the traditions of the Prophet and in relation to the social milieu in which they lived. 'Their whole attempt...in rationalizing the customary practices, is essentially to resolve the inherent tension between custom and the general and broad principles of the sharia' (p. 311). In this regard, 'The two interacted on each other' and, 'The result was the creative product, the substantive law of tenure' (ibid.).

This substantial law of tenure represents no common ground. Abu Hanifa was totally uncompromising concerning sharecropping and condemned it as un-Islamic and bordering on being speculative (*gharar*). Malik and Al-Shafi'i departed from the method of reasoning of Abu Hanifa but arrived at the same conclusion about the issue. However, Abu Yusuf who was an adviser to Haroon Al-Rashid (786–809) made an attempt to validate a custom which had already reached a high level of development. His attitude towards the problem was that if they were 'not called into question on the grounds of the interests of the Umma and the spirit of Islam, the existing arrangements and practices of tenure must continue to function as part of the general law of the Empire' (p. 325). Ahmad Ibn Hanbal (d. 855–856) applied the method of *modaraba* to the question of land and concluded that a third or a quarter of the crop claimed by the landlord was valid in Islam. [Abu Hanifa, Malik, Al-Shafi'i, and Hanbal are the leading jurists in the Sunni tradition.]

It is quite obvious that the Islamic law concerning land tenure is evolutionary in nature and is subject to development on the basis of the criteria of justice and equity. Ibn Taymmiya (d.1327), for example, emphasized the role of *qiyas* (deductive reasoning) about the matter. The main issue for him, was not that the Prophet had imposed a ban on primitive aleatory tenure system, but about the examination of the reason for this action. The

Prophet's action, according to him, was prompted by the fact that the system was prone to exploitation of the tenant by the landlord. The system of *muzara'a* could be made acceptable if it was based on the contractual arrangement between the landlord and the tenant for sharing profit and loss from the enterprise. Although he arrived at the same conclusion as Abu Yusuf, he made explicit an underlying assumption which runs as a common thread in the casuistic writings of the jurists, that the landlord and the tenant were equal partners in the use of land. This assumption was never fully realized in the history of Islam, and today in most cases including that of Pakistan the tenants and sharecroppers remain totally dependent on land and are even in many cases reduced to the status of subject peasantry.

From the Jurists to Islamic Economics

The mainstream thinking in Islamic economics is based on a priori assumption that individual property right is an integral part of an Islamic economy. It is, however, embellished by the concept of the divine system. Using the Qur'anic verses such as II:284 (Unto Allah whatsoever is in the heaven and whatsoever is in the earth) and XXII:65 (Hasn't thou not seen how Allah hath made all that is in the earth subservient unto you), the Islamic economists emphasize the notion of trusteeship of man and man's ultimate responsibility to God. The policy implications of this approach are not clear, however, because all the issues relating to property must nevertheless be decided by the man-made laws.

The rules of economic behaviour in an Islamic economy for Naqvi (1994), for example, would require that the institution of private property be regulated as part of the Islamicization programme in the country, including feudal holdings (p. 146). Sheikh (1961) would restrict land holdings to the size suitable for self-cultivation only (p.□181). He rejects Maudoodi's *laissez faire* approach to land and is critical of his defence of landlordism (pp. 163–81). Mannan (1986) is of the view that modern landlordism was not present in the pre-Islamic days or afterwards. He does not favour the idea of leasing land, as this system in any form leads to great injustice to the tenant (p. 81).

The divine system then which the Islamic economists emphasize concerning the role of private property may allow some leeway for what may be called populist or state-populist approaches (Behdad 1992). The *laissez faire* point of view, however, is dominant. Support for this point of view was provided by the Council of Islamic Ideology (CII) in its rulings on the various cases examined by it, and by the Federal Shariat Court (FSC) and the Shariat Appellate Court Bench of the Supreme Court (SAB) during the last twenty years. These institutions of course are the legacy of General Ziaul Haq as part of the amended constitution promulgated by him.

Zulfikar Ali Bhutto had promoted his land reform through the Land Reform Act which was passed by the National Assembly in 1977, the year in which his government was dismissed by General Ziaul Haq as the martial law administrator. During the short interregnum between the introduction of the act and the departure of Bhutto government, the implementation of land reform was quite modest, as was the land reform introduced during the period of Ayub Khan. It nevertheless caused considerable opposition from the landlords as they perceived it to be more threatening to their interests. Also, the administration of the act was seriously flawed because of political factors and administrative problems.

The crux of the controversy became the right of pre-emption by the tenants and it has been carefully examined in a recent article (Kennedy 1993). The CII decided that tenants had no such rights. The FSC and SAB in their respective decisions declared these rights as un-Islamic.

It is obvious that as long as the ulama keep an upper hand in their right to decide what is or is not un-Islamic, and as long as the opinions of classical jurists are given the status of being the final word on Islamic law, the scope for reconstructing the economy are limited. This is notwithstanding the claims made by some Islamic economists regarding welfare state and distributive justice as the hallmark of an Islamic economy.

The Laws of Inheritance

The rigidity of Islamic jurisprudence is best exemplified by the Islamic laws of inheritance. There is no doubt that Islam pioneered an effective measure to promote distribution of entitlements among the heirs. The basic source of the law is the concept of the 'Qur'anic heirs' which, while recognizing some pre-Islamic customs, introduces important innovations such as recognition of rights of women (verses IV:7-12; IV:176). The law further evolved in the context of the traditions of the Prophet, and the reasoning of the jurists concerning this and other aspects of family life in Islam. The structure of the law of course has the basic principles of sharia as the guiding force, but interpretation of these principles is an important matter for *fiqah* [jurisprudence]. This process of interpretation involves the issue of consensus and the place of consensus in the changing social and economic life of the country. The ulama tend to resist any change in the law which may modify the consensus of the classical jurists.

In the Sunni tradition, the law as developed on the basis of the Qur'anic injunctions relies on the concept of agnate, '...individual of either sex so related to the propositus that there is no intervening female link' (Carrol 1983: 630). It means that a daughter is an agnate but the daughter's child is not; and the son is an agnate as are also the son's sons or daughters. The explicit focus of the Sunni law is a family system in which the male heirs play an important role in promoting and maintaining the family traditions. It is obvious that this interpretation of the Qu'ranic injunction evolved in the context of a specific socio-economic environment.

The fact that the Shia law of inheritance differs from the Sunni law and it refuses to afford any special place or privileged position to the agnatic relatives indicates clearly that the Qu'ranic injunctions are open to interpretation. A major difference between the two laws, therefore, is that in a situation where there is only a daughter as a legitimate heir of the deceased, she is entitled to two-thirds to one-half share in the Sunni law, depending upon other claimants, but she will get the full share in accordance with the Shia law. This difference has significant implications from the point of view of reconstruction of the law in the context of modern times. The Shia system gives an obvious and consistent priority to the immediate family and makes no provision for 'tribal' relatives, except in the total absence of any claimants who may be more closely related to the deceased. It does not mean that the Shia system should replace the Sunni system because that in itself would not resolve the issue. Both systems are very much alike and similar in their androcentric approach to family and inheritance. A case can be made, however, for creating a new law so that the best parts of each could be combined into the revised system—a process of *talfiq* (Anderson 1965: 353, refers to it in a different context). This process would not be enough to bring about the real change, however, and additional steps would be required towards a re-examination of the consensual opinions of the classical jurists.

There have been some attempts made to introduce reforms in the law in several Muslim countries. Anderson (1965) examines in detail the major reforms effected in Egypt, Syra, Tunisia, and Morocco. These reforms represent modest steps in the right direction from the point of view of the above criteria. In Pakistan, an effort was made to deal with the problem of exclusion of grandchildren from the estate of the grandfather by the survival of the uncle. In 1961, a provision in the Muslim Family Laws Ordinance was introduced towards this end. It has been a very controversial amendment because it weakens the principle of agnate priority as required by the Sunni legal tradition. Under the amendment, the daughter of the predeceased son would exclude the brother of her grandfather. The fabric of joint-family system has considerably weakened in Pakistan. This kind of opposition, therefore, should be construed less in terms of family solidarity and more as an indication of how strong vested interests have developed around the old tradition.

Conclusion

I have focused my discussion on the Sunni law of inheritance because it is the dominant system in Pakistan. Both the Shia and the Sunni laws rightly claim to be the most comprehensive laws as compared to the laws in other cultures. Except for the Hindu law, not many other laws of succession are so permeated with religion in them. The Sunni law is a unified code and it gives the appearance of carrying behind it complete unanimity of juristic opinions. This is not the case. There are shades of opinions and there are substantive differences among the jurists. For example, Abu Yusuf who was a disciple of the Hanafi system, disagreed with opinions of Abu Hanifa, as noted above. In fact the law is quite eclectic and accommodates sectarian differences. It is nevertheless rigid because only the classical jurists may be invoked in order to support a change in the law, a status which none of them ever claimed. They were formulating opinions in light of the Qur'anic principles and the traditions of the Prophet, but they knew that they were directly influenced by the social milieu in which they lived.

The purpose of the Qur'an in defining heirs was mainly to correct a serious injustice which was in practice in Arabia of that period with regard to women, and to protect their rights. The task of the Prophetic mission in this regard was to awaken the community to this new reality. This pioneering reform had a far-reaching impact on the Medina society, and the tension arising from this change contributed to the controversy about *hijab* (Mernissi 1991: 85ff.). The share of the woman as compared to the male heirs may seem incongruous in modern times. Iqbal, for example, examines the issue and concludes that there is no material difference between the respective total inheritance received by the daughter and the son. The daughter receives her share as a daughter, as a mother and a wife, and has right over her dower-money. The son must, on the other hand, take full responsibility for maintaining his wife throughout her life (1950: 170). It seems, however, that in terms of the possible total amounts inherited the share of the son would probably exceed that of the daughter. There is further discussion about the rights of women with regard to inheritance in Chapter 7 below.

The prospects of reinterpreting the place of the Qur'anic heirs with a view to removing or narrowing the gender factor are not very bright in the near future. Perhaps the first most important step in that direction would be to bring about social change in which entitlements in name also become a reality, so that women have the right and the opportunity to exercise independent judgement about the use and disposition of their shares. From the point of view of the law of inheritance as a whole, the principle of 'per stirpes' distribution as provided in the Shia law would seem to have greater possibilities of being in harmony with the emerging nuclear family system than dividing the claims according to the criterion of agnatic heirs.

There are other inequities in the laws of inheritance as they are practiced in modern Pakistan. No serious studies are available on this subject. The anecdotal evidence, however, indicates that, in practice, the Muslim society of Pakistan has never been ready to accept the principle of giving shares to all claimants included among the Qur'anic heirs [as hab-ul-far'iz], and is very selective about the rights of residuaries. There is, therefore, considerable hypocracy about application of rules concerning agnatic heirs. Every effort is made to keep property as concentrated in fewer hands of the powerful members of the family as possible. In the Western countries, there is a very clear mechanism to probate the will and dispose of the estate of the deceased according to the law. Of course, there are property disputes but in general the system seems to work. In Pakistan, will has a very limited role under the Islamic law. The purpose of this restriction is to protect the interests of all lawful heirs. It seems, however, that other means are used to frustrate the objective of the law. There are no built-in safeguards in the legal framework of the country to make sure that the question of the disposition of property is handled in accordance with the Islamic rules of justice. Also, there is no satisfactory procedure by which the inventory of the property—movable as well as immovable— is duly registered and divided as required by the laws of inheritance, without invoking the need for litigation to settle the matter. There are many loopholes in the system as it exists today. Not many can afford to fight against the injustices created by these loopholes and, therefore, they must suffer their fate in silence.

The above anecdotal evidence is supported by the few court rulings concerning cases which were brought to that level, and these rulings involve the situation of women, though the principles underlying these rulings would have general applicability. The usual explanation given to exclude female heirs from inheritance is the plea that they have voluntarily relinquished their rights in favour of the male heirs. There are some indications that the courts have become skeptical of this explanation. It has been held, for example, by these courts that the inheritance of the female claimant remains intact irrespective of the actual control exercised by the male heir, and notwithstanding the mutation of revenue records in his favour (Malik, Ayesha, 1997).

The question of property rights is related to the opinions and views of the classical jurists and the place of these jurists in modern times. It seems that the ulama are overwhelmingly in favour of the status quo on this matter. Their entire focus is only on the question of riba, which has become a fetish with them. Also the claims of the Islamic economists about the role of the laws of inheritance in promoting a better distribution of wealth would remain seriously lacking in its meaning until a comprehensive study is made about these laws. Any reform necessarily must begin with a simultaneous examination of the criteria of justice and benevolence (*adl* and *ah'san*) in modern economic thinking, and the need to accommodate these criteria in jurisprudence. There is no evidence to indicate that the importance for such a reform is being felt in the country. An observation made concerning the case of Iran is quite relevant for Pakistan: 'The Islamic jurisprudential tradition is more forcefully explicit in the defence of private property than many Islamic social reformers are willing to realize' (Behdad 1992: 96).

Appendix

Sharecropping and Economic Theory

The position of economists concerning sharecropping has undergone a significant change in the history of economic thought. From Adam Smith to Marshall, this institution was disapproved categorically. For Smith, 'It could never... be the interest of cultivators to lay out in further improvement of the land, any part of the little stock which they might save from their own share of the produce, because the lord, who laid down nothing was to get one-half of whatever it produced' (1937: 367). Smith then is condemning a system in which the landlord receives his share of the total produce in exchange for permitting a cultivator to use his land; and presumably he is not a co-sharer in any of the activity related to cultivation such as capital, seeds, plough, etc.

Marshall in his Principles (1961 edition) dealt with the question of land tenure and examined the sharecropping system then practised in the New World in which labour and capital combined their efforts as against the English system of rental arrangement. Under the former, the cultivator would be free to cultivate but it would not be to his interest to apply any doses the total return to which was less than twice enough to reward him; he would thus cultivate far less intensively than on the English plan (p. 644). In a footnote on page 643, Marshall suggests that the tenant's share could vary from one-third where the land was rich to four-fifths where there was much labour and the landlord's share was modest. In a footnote on page 644, he lays the foundation of a more precise explanation of the tenant's share with reference to the well-known Marshallian geometry.

The advantages of sharecropping are considerable, concludes Marshall, when the holdings are very small, the tenants poor, and the landlord not averse to taking trouble about small things. It is not suitable for holdings large enough to give scope to the enterprise of an able and responsible tenant (p. 645).

With the advent of neoclassical analysis, there has been a growing literature on the subject. In 1968, Cheung offered an analysis in defence of sharecropping and claimed that in the framework of certain assumptions relating to private property rights, the system would compare favourably with that of fixed rent in allocative efficiency. This claim by Cheung has led to further discussion on the subject which seems to be continuing. Badhuri (1973), Ghatak (1976) and Scandizzo (1979) disagree with Cheung and hold the view that sharecropping as an interlocked phenomenon involving capital, labour, and availability of credit for the tenant seemed to allow the landlord to extract the maximum surplus from the land, resulting in indebtedness of the tenant. The other critics of Cheung such as Bardhan (1978) and Srinivisan (1979) refute the involuntary nature of the extraction of surplus because they assume that the credit market would be competitive.

Other contributions on the subject, however, have broadly supported Cheung's conclusions in their models (esp. Newbury 1975), all asserting that the much maligned institution of share tenancy has in fact distinct advantages (see the review article by Quibria and Rashid 1984). An empirical study relating to Pakistan (Nabi 1986) shows that, based on Khanewal subdivision of the province of Punjab, the landlords in general specify the terms of the contract, encourage the sharecropper to adopt new techniques and that sharecropping does not produce results in output less favourable than other kinds of tenancy contracts.

The neoclassical analysis is based on two important assumptions. First, the cultivator is able to act like an independent agent in the market. This would depend on the extent to which the economy has moved away from the feudal structure, or even semi-feudal capitalist mode of production. Accident of birth, both in the case of the landlord and the tenant may determine to great extent the relation between them and the place of custom and competition in this relationship.

The second assumption relates to the questions concerning Pareto optimality, Coase theorem, and other related neoclassical tools of analysis. This matter has been discussed in Chapter 3 above.

The ethical issue remains, however: who controls the land, who may reap the benefits from it, and who should bear the cost of agricultural activity. This ethical issue impinges on religion but is not confined to it. There are socio-economic factors which must be examined from the point of view of national social welfare. Further studies will be required, on a more extensive basis, to assess the neoclassical conclusions and relevance for Pakistan of the empirical data relating to other countries. The issue cannot be settled by establishing religious sanctity of sharecropping alone by invoking opinions of some classical jurists of Islam.

CHAPTER 6

The Question of the Islamic Economic System

The 1949 Objectives Resolution declared, *inter alia,* that Pakistan would follow the principles of democracy, freedom, equality, tolerance, and social justice as enunciated by Islam. In his speech introducing the Resolution, Liaquat Ali Khan, the then Prime Minister, emphasized that Islam had a role to play in building the Pakistani society in which life would be free from want and rich in freedom (Mahmood 1975: 17). In 1956, the constitution explicitly guaranteed the right of citizens to acquire, hold, and dispose of property (section 8-b) and, subject to powers of the state to regulate, the right to pursue any profession or occupation and to conduct any lawful trade or business. This principle was incorporated in the 1962 Constitution and became an integral part of the 1973 Constitution of the country (Mahmood: 812ff).

The infrastructure for a capitalist economy, therefore, based on market mechanism, was solidly built in the constitution of Pakistan. It was fully recognized in all constitutional debates. There were controversies about the nature of Pakistan as an Islamic state, with reference to the role of the head of the state and of the legislative body. However, the same groups of ulama who vigorously promoted their views about these matters, seemed to have approved the evolution and the shape of the economy as envisaged by the constitution. The 1973 Constitution, of course, declared that exploitation in all forms was to be eliminated, that state was to provide basic necessities of life for all citizens and to prevent concentration of wealth in the hands of a few and, further, to ensure equitable rights between employers and employees as well as landlords and tenants (Mahmood: 809–818). These aims were in line with the programme of the Pakistan People's Party of Zulfikar Ali Bhutto. In order, however, to build consensus on the Constitution from other parties and the ulama, specific Islamic provisions were included in its part ix, in order to transform the existing capitalist economy of Pakistan into an Islamic economy. These provisions became the basis of the Islamicization programme of General Ziaul Haq, as discussed in Chapter 2 above, amending and enlarging the 1973 Constitution in order to build an Islamic economic system in the country, as interpreted by him and his political allies.

The Origins of Capitalism Revisited

The main infrastructure of Pakistan fits in with the objectives of capitalism: a national system in which there is private ownership of means of production and, in which capital, labour, and resources are linked together through the market mechanism. The questions of what to produce, how to produce, how much to produce, and for whom are determined by the market, subject to the limits set by state regulation.

The nineteenth century industrialization in Western Europe resulted in rapid economic growth in that region. It was also the period in which the ideology of *laissez-faire* prevailed. What is meant by this ideology is open to several meanings. As an economic philosophy, it provided a sanction to dismantle the existing institutions and to build a new society based on self-interest propelled only by the actions of man and his physical universe. The derived laws of market economy were given the authority of nature

(Dalton 1974: 44ff). It also brought in its wake the inequalities of income and rise of pauperism. There were socialist responses to this development, Marxian as well as democratic. After the Great Depression, a new reformed capitalism emerged, inspired largely by Keynes, from the New Deal in the USA to the rise of social welfare as a function of the state, especially in Western Europe.

The development of the European capitalism was fostered by the norms, values, and beliefs of individual actors as well as the societies in which they played their role. However, a causal connection between religion and capitalism requires caution as indicated by the extended controversy around the contributions of Weber (see for example Samuelsson 1957). In his book, *Why has Japan 'Succeeded'?* (1982), Michio Morishima suggests that a flexible combination of ethical systems, not a single religion, contributed to Japan's impressive economic growth. The market mechanism as understood in the Anglo-American model did not play a crucial role, particularly with regard to the use of labour (pp. 117–18). For him, it is a model of autochthenous growth of Japanese capitalism which was essentially nationalistic, paternalistic, and anti-individualistic, and in which Confucianism made humans aware that apart from making money they must do something for society and the country. The Meiji Revolution was a catalyst and it was the result of a perpetual awareness by the Japanese elite of the overwhelming cultural and technological gap between Japan and the foreign West (p. 195). Morishima presents an intriguing hypothesis and underlines the necessity for alternative explanations of economic behaviour. A question arises, for example, concerning the economic conditions in contemporary China and its potential for growth in the nineteenth century world economy (Moulder 1977). China suffered a deep encroachment by the Western powers while Japan enjoyed a relative degree of isolation during the critical period of its growth (pp. 92–7). Also, the Japanese military adventures in the neighbouring countries played a role in stimulating industrial growth in that country. In Wallerstein's framework (1974 and 1980), these two countries remained outside the newly developing *European* world economy, dragged only bit by bit in the colonial network.

Weber, who associated the rise of Western Europe's modern economy to teachings of Calvin and Luther, also regarded Confucianism responsible for China's backwardness. It is an irony of interpretation of economic history that the success of East Asian economies during the seventies and eighties was ascribed to Confucian values as one of the important factors. Also, it is important to understand that the leading sectors in East and South-East Asian economies have been family-oriented conglomerates, with no resemblance to family-owned or family-originated enterprises in the United States. The founders of these business enterprises have been, nevertheless, individuals, creating a climate of cooperation among close family members. It is, therefore, still relevant to ask what motivates a person to pursue entrepreneurial activity and it is a difficult question to answer. A positive religious belief may serve as an added incentive, but it is generally recognized in the literature, that individuals tend to compartmentalize conflicting values in their economic goals (Belshaw 1964; Hagen 1962; Rostow 1971). There has to be some harmony, however, between individual goals and those of the relevant groups and of the society. With reference to the new industrial age, Galbraith observes that 'the relationship between society at large and an organisation must be consistent with the relations of the organization to the individual' (Galbraith: 159). Unlike the feudal situation where compulsion and tradition compel the liege men to accompany the lord for his military duty, in a market economy, the goals tend to coincide around pecuniary gains and maximization of income and welfare. Once the pecuniary compensation is accomplished, other motives take over. (pp. 161–2). This observation seems to have some historical relevance, for the early period of capitalism, not only for the new industrial state. And it must work as a cementing force for family enterprises as well. Consistency may not be perfect, and in fact there may be occasional tension between the goals at two levels, but the opportunities must be there to perceive for the individuals and to participate in them. It is a reciprocal link in which both the economic and non-economic institutions play their roles.

The Economic Functions under Capitalism

The objective of the capitalist system is to provide for the use of resources in a manner as to maximize output at minimum cost, to encourage full utilization of these resources and to establish a mechanism for distribution of rewards of the productive activity.

Pakistan is a case of a developing capitalism, a hybrid of traditional and modern. In the agricultural sector of the economy, broadly following Gottlieb's classification of economic systems, the feudal and the landlord modes of production coexist in the economy (Gottlieb 1984). The feudal mode, again following Gottlieb, may be defined as a situation in which the labourer has the obligation to give money, labour or products to the master, over and above his subsistence, and his ability to move is restricted. It should be pointed out that feudalism in Pakistan is not a prototype of the well-known medieval European institution, but it has perhaps the worst features of power relations of that system. In the landlord mode there may be an owner-cultivator or an absentee landlord, depending on the size of his holding. The social subordination of the tenant to landlord may be bourgeois or it might have some feudal elements imposed by custom and lack of alternative opportunities. Gottlieb suggests that the landlord class by virtue of its property stake, higher incomes, etc. becomes a political and social power in rural society (pp. 71–2), and this is quite relevant for Pakistan.

The capitalist mode of production in the country is characterized by the use of loaned or equity capital for profits in industry and commerce, by landowners for developing real estate, by labour working for wage and by the suppliers of raw materials, equipment etc. for agreed price. The informal sector, consisting of entrepreneur-workers, or entrepreneurs with small scale productive activity with assistance of hired labour, does not have the complexity of the larger enterprises. The capitalist sector include profit- and loss-sharing and *modaraba*. The corporate mode includes the managers, shareholders, and directors and it is still a small and growing sector of the economy.

It is a multimodal economic system, with an expanding share of its gross domestic product originating from the capitalist sector. The forces which will determine the intra-modal efficiency and productivity, as well as inter-modal use of resources, will depend on the level of economic growth of the economy as a whole. The extent to which the rate of unemployment and expanding population will outpace economic growth, to that extent the inter-sectoral mobility will be hindered, resulting in an under-employed economic system. The model of 'unlimited supply of labour' (Lewis 1954) bringing about a complete structural change in the economy by using the large reservoir of labour would not work in the country because one of its key implicit assumptions about modernization of the agricultural sector has not been fulfilled. Pakistan's agriculture is stuck in a limbo of economic transitions. It has strong links with the modern national and international commerce, but it also has mixed and contradictory modes of production, ranging from feudal to peasant-proprietor. The model of course has raised other theoretical and empirical controversies which may not be relevant for the present argument. There is also the phenomenon of serious under-employment in urban areas of the country. One does not encounter the pavement-dwellers in Pakistan as in some megacities in other parts of Asia, but 'fragmentation' of work, as pointed out by the well-known British economist, Joan Robinson, in another context, is a highly relevant index of the problem in the country. The reality manifests itself in many ways, such as five porters wanting to carry a piece of luggage at the country's airports.

Production in the various sectors of the economy will be determined by the economic-technical criteria. If a producer is a practising Muslim, for example, he may bring to bear considerations of his belief by avoiding production of certain goods. This in itself does not change the nature of his capitalist activity. It may limit or bar the production or consumption of goods disallowed on religious grounds. The system does not become transformed into an Islamic economic system.

Capitalism and Islamic Economics

The Islamic economists claim, however, that there is a distinct Islamic economic system. It may resemble capitalism in many respects, but its aims and objectives are different. Private property, for example, is a core assumption of capitalism. In the Islamic economic system, it is claimed, private property is only a trust because sovereignty belongs to God and man's duty is to pursue his goals according to God's will. In operational terms, this behavioural norm for the *homo Islamicus*, as already discussed in the previous chapter has in fact very little legal significance. As far as the productive activity is concerned, ethical considerations as a behavioural norm are common to all cultures. In order to cope with lapses in the market mechanism, there is a strong body of literature in all capitalist countries aimed at promoting and maintaining fair prices for goods, services and factors of production. How invulnerable is the pursuit of self-interest under capitalism is a difficult question to answer. Will it be harnessed more effectively in an Islamic system is by no means a clear issue. As a moral question, it is very much alive in the capitalist societies as well.

It is said that the Islamic economic system would be characterized by interest-free financial system. The Islamicization of the banks in Pakistan, as discussed in Chapter 4 above has not succeeded in abolishing interest, only in providing the banking system with subterfuges. In fact the theoretical foundation of the concept is tenuous, and in juristic literature it is subject to interpretation. The profit-sharing institutions such as *modaraba*, however, which emphasize a form of equity investment are quite consistent with the capitalist system. But, as mentioned in Chapter 4 above, they provide no mechanism to identify the risk taken by an individual subscriber of capital. Similarly, the introduction of a compulsory *zakat* fund in 1980, under the Sunni tradition, has not changed the capitalist structure of the country. It may or may not serve as an incentive against hoarding. The evidence so far is inconclusive in terms of its impact on capital formation in the country. Also, the flat rate of *zakat* in a small community might serve as a vehicle for providing benefits to those who are in need, without affecting in any significant manner the economic interests of members of the community as a whole. In a larger society, as pointed out by Kuran (1989), where income and wealth levels as well as entitlements are unevenly spread out, it would serve as a regressive tax.

The third feature of the Islamic economic system is the laws of inheritance. These laws do not relate to the issue of the economic system as such with reference to the capitalist mode of production. They impinge, however, on the question of the distribution of wealth. They may help or hinder the economic activity in the country. The predominant Sunni law has a clear gender bias, and it may be in conflict with the evolving nuclear family system. It is also faced with practical problems which seem to compromise its objectives. These issue have been examined in Chapter 6 above.

What then is the *raison dietre* for the Islamic economic system? Perhaps the main inspiration for search for this system is related to the emergence of independent Muslim states in the post-World War II era. Islam was being adapted so that its universalistic spirit could be harnessed to promote nationalism. The focus was on national economic goals which must be defined in the new context. With the resurgence of political Islam, further impetus was given to identifying a distinct economic system consistent with the ideal of the Islamic state. Gellner's classification (1985, Introduction, pp. 1–9) gives a perspective to this phenomenon. He identifies three processes at work in the modern world: industrialization, nationalism, and reformism. Industrialization includes diffusion of modern technology and it extends beyond the narrow question of the methods of production. Reformism is a tendency towards scripturalist-puritanism, and nationalism in creating a broader identity weakens local mediation in order to establish a new anonymous collectivity (p. 3). In Europe these three transformations were connected but were separated by a couple of centuries. In the Muslim world, the phenomenon is taking place almost simultaneously.

Why should the emergent puritanism be linked with nationalism? A plausible explanation, according to Gellner, is the rise of the new socio-economic order replacing the old in an impersonal manner (p. 7), connecting the larger identity through religious tradition which is indigenous, not imported, and is authentic. Unlike the European reformism, however, which was linked with the use of the local vernacular to spread the Word, in the Muslim tradition the religious message is delivered in the language which for the non-Arab countries, is associated with the far-flung culture with which the scripture is linked (p. 4). This point has considerable relevance with regard to the Arabic vocabulary which abounds in Islamic economics and which in the vernaculars of Pakistan society, for example, would carry different connotations. In Urdu, *riba* is translated as *sood*, but the Urdu term has a special meaning in the context of the South Asian society, as mentioned in Chapter 3 above. It seems that the non-Arab Muslim nationalism faces two-fold dilemma. First, which it shares with the Arabs, it must examine the socio-economic context in which a Qur'anic injunction is revealed and then relate it to modern times. And secondly, it must interpret the injunction in terms of the local conditions. It is a quest for a suitable economic policy, a new solution to the new problems created by national economic development, and inspired by the values of the religion.

From an historical perspective, Islamic values were not in conflict with the spirit of capitalism. Rodinson (1973) has examined the issue thoroughly. The socio-economic function—the rational use of commercial and finance capital—is clearly in evidence in the early Muslim period. Wherever, the current juristic interpretation of the Qur'anic injunction seemed to be in conflict with the reality of economic life, a variety of subterfuges were used to overcome the obstacle (Rodinson, chapters 3 & 4). The underdevelopment of the Muslim world, Rodinson argues (chap. 5), cannot be ascribed to the teachings of Islam. Using the Marxist dictum, he suggests that ideology shows itself to be a great deal less powerful than the social situation (p. 157).

Could the Muslim world move towards establishing a socialist economic order as an alternative to capitalism, asks Rodinson? For him, capitalism and socialism are not contradictory, because socialism in the Marxian tradition is dialectically derived from capitalism. It is in the relations of production, and not in the mode of production, that they represent differences. Rodinson holds the view that the scope for using Islam as a 'utopian' ideology for a socialist order and of ignoring the factors such as sanctity of private property is not very bright (p. 214ff), though he seems to feel that the choice of socialism would produce a more just society in the Muslim world (chap. 4). A Muslim economist (Jomo 1977) disagrees with Rodinson and suggests that he tends to underestimate the revolutionary potential of Islam and its possible compatibility with socialism (p. 247). The mainstream Islamic thinking, however, is hostile to socialism and so are the Islamic economists.

Would a truly Islamic alternative have evolved, had industrialization not taken place first in Western Europe, and what pattern would it have taken in the Muslim society? It is not an easy question to answer as one would have to make hypothetical assumptions about possible scenarios. Going beyond Weber, it would nevertheless be important to identify the obstacles which prevented the socio-economic formation from expanding to the stage of full-blown capitalist development. Sami Zubaida (1972) analyzed this issue a year before Rodinson's book became available in the English translation. Zubaida focused on the stages in the development of Islam from the formative period from the Prophet to the Caliphs, from caliphate to imperial dynasties of Umayyad and Abbasid rulers, to the fragmentation of the empire. It was not the attitudes or ideologies inherent in Islam which inhibit the development of a capitalist economy, but the political position of the merchant classes in Islamic societies. Unlike their equivalents in Western European medieval cities, the Middle East merchant classes did not develop the bases for class political organization and autonomy (p. 324). This point of view underlines the socio-structural factors which determine the relationship of the bourgeoisie to the military ruling class and to the state.

Abu-Lughod has examined this question in a broader context with reference to the world system before the rise of European hegemony during AD 1250–1350. There were many similarities between the East—consisting mainly of China, South Asia, and the Middle East— and the West in that period (1989, chapter 1). These similarities existed in the institution of money and credit, mechanism for pooling capital, and for distribution of risk, and with regard to the accumulation of merchant wealth. What distinguished the two regions was that the thirteenth century Europe lagged behind the East. In the sixteenth century, however, Europe pulled ahead when the 'Orient' was temporarily in disarray (p. 18). The crucial fact, underlined by Abu-Lughod is, that the 'Fall of the East' preceded the 'Rise of the West' (chapter 11). There was no unity in culture, religion, or economic institutional arrangements prevailing in the earlier incipient world system. 'No particular culture seems to have had a monopoly over either technological or social inventiveness' (p. 354). This view may seem to contradict Zubaida's position concerning the lagging performance of the Middle East in its capitalist development. Abu-Lughod emphasizes that during Abbasid period, capitalism flowered (p. 217). She refers to the growth of law and practice relating to partnerships, contracts and the commenda agreements, with reference to Udovitch (1970). She describes the vibrant activity in agriculture, trade and industry in Fustat-Cairo which had reached a peak in 1294–1340 during the reign of Sultan al-Nasir Muhammad (p. 224ff). The Mongol invasion weakened the economic infrastructure and Black Death gave a severe blow to the system. According to Abu-Lughod, then, there is no inherent historical necessity, in other respects, that would have prevented cultures in the eastern region from becoming the progenitors of a modern world system (p. 12).

There is, nevertheless, some convergence in the two views. Both agree that Weber's theses concerning religion and secular action are irrelevant regarding the main problem. Both use Goitein (1966) for important references to interpret the economic trends in the Middle East during the period under consideration. For Zubaida, the essential issue is to identify the reasons why economic activism, which played a crucial role in the European economy, failed in the context of the Middle East. 'By all accounts, trade and crafts prospered in period of imperial centralization. Merchants accumulated great fortunes and enjoyed high status...' (p. 326). Also, the state provided facilities for transport and protection over wide areas of the old world. The political position and influence of rich merchants was purely individual and personal, however. '*As a class* they did not develop institutional or collective bases of power' (p. 327, italics in text).

A general conclusion from this observation is possible in the context of modern times. The question of relations between the state and the entrepreneurial class has important bearing on the development of an economy, whether it is growth-promoting or growth-hindering, and whether or not their interests converge regarding economic goals. The experience of the East Asian economies during the seventies and the eighties lends a great deal of support to this conclusion.

The central theme of Islamic economics is to create a just society in which the emphasis will be on social welfare of all members of the society, and the objective will be to control sharp inequalities of income. It is assumed that the economic system will be an integral part of the Islamic state. There is some discussion about the areas of state intervention in promoting the goals of the just society (Naqvi 1994), The main question concerning the relations between the state and the Islamic economy is generally ignored in the literature, because a great deal of emphasis is placed on individual action—the behavioural norms for the pious Muslim. Consequently, the Islamic economists manage to stay at a comfortable abstract level with their emphasis on the system as they perceive it, and comparing it with the reality of Western capitalism. The current economic problems facing the Muslim society and the need for suitable policies to correct them are never seriously discussed. This approach is based on the assumption that when the principle is established, the process will automatically follow. Kuran (1989: 176ff) has referred to this problem in his analysis of the Islamic economic system. This question is further explored in the next section.

The Principles and the Processes of Justice

The objectives of Islamic justice as envisaged by the classical jurists are clearly stated in the relevant literature: to obey the injunctions for *halal* and *haram* (the permissible and the forbidden), to fulfil duties and respect contracts, and to contribute to the general good of the society. What is the relation between justice and revelation and between voluntary action and Divine Will are questions which have been debated vigorously in the history of Islamic jurisprudence and have been lucidly examined recently by Khadduri in his comprehensive study on the subject (1984). The discussion in this section relies heavily on his contribution.

Ghazzali, who started with a position giving each, revelation as well as reason, a place in human action, emphasized in his later life the supremacy of mystical experience over reason (pp. 114–15). Al-Razi was deeply committed, on the other hand to reason and was of the view that Divine Will could be attained only through reason (p. 116). These are two examples of abstract philosophical opinions which give an insight into the thinking of early Islamic jurists. The question of legal and social justice, however, poses a different challenge. Khadduri distinguishes between what he calls the substantive and the procedural aspects of justice. The lawmakers decide how much justice may be contained in the substance of the law, the rule of right and wrong. Procedural justice relates to the degree of impartiality in the application of the law. The historical experience indicates that the emphasis was placed more on the reputation of the judge than the system of justice (p. 145). A gap developed between the two concepts and the procedural justice proved inadequate to fulfil the requirements of the Islamic legal system (p. 158). Legal devices (*hiyal*), forms of casuistry and councils of complaints were developed to establish equity and to cope with the inadequacy of procedures (p. 156).

In the area of social justice, the problem is even more intractable, as it underlines the social customs and habits apart from the norms and values of the law. The modern Islamicists emphasize the latter in order to Islamicize the former. Among the classical jurists, Ibn Taymiyya tried to maintain a balance between idealism of the deductive approach and the realism of the inductive (p. 179). For Ibn Khaldun, the secular force of *asabiya* was the source of dynamics of a great society—a third category of states in which a mixture of secular and religious laws prevailed (p. 187). In the other two categories, respectively, public order is derived from revelational source but it is dependent on laws laid down by man.

Conclusion

The purpose of this chapter has been to examine the question of the Islamic economic system as defined by the Islamicists. The issue really is concerning suitable economic policy for Pakistan, a comprehensive policy which reflects the norms and values of Pakistan as a Muslim society, and is consistent with its goal for a sustainable economic development. This cannot be accomplished by attempts to transplant the institutions of medieval Islam. The problem of elimination of riba, for example, falls in this category. The system of compulsory collection of *zakat* was introduced in 1980 and the purpose was to establish a national administration for the disbursement of the fund in accordance with the objectives as defined by the classical jurists. The fund seems to have fallen short of its goals (Mohammad 1991) and it is not clear if its distribution reached those who needed it the most to meet their minimum requirements. The anecdotal evidence indicates that there is a serious problem of mismanagement of the fund. Similarly, the laws of inheritance, as they have been practised in the country, have not shown any real impact on the distribution of wealth in the country.

In order to establish a just society in Pakistan, both the substantive and the procedural aspects of economic policies, and of the legal system in general, would require a careful attention from Islamic scholars, legal experts, and social scientists in Pakistan.

CHAPTER 7

Women and Islam[1]

There is complete agreement in Pakistan that Islam protects the rights of women. The question is about how to define these rights and how to interpret the reality. What role women can play, for example, in the economic development of the Islamic Republic of Pakistan is still largely an unsettled question. The economic planning authorities have usually emphasized an urgent need for a more effective participation of women in the modern sector of the economy. The traditionalist religious leaders, however, do not want women to work outside the home or hold public office, because 'In the eyes of Islam a woman is very precious and valuable, therefore she has to remain indoors where she could be hidden and guarded, just as precious and valuable assets are guarded and kept in safes, strong-rooms and vaults for safe keeping, so that they do not fall into the hands of unauthorized persons' (Imran 1990: 76). Some conservative writers, however, would permit women to take up part-time jobs—or full-time positions when their maternal or domestic functions are over—in those areas of activity where they are likely to have no direct contact with male strangers (Siddiqi 1996).

The position of the modernists differs from that of the ulama and their conservative supporters. They believe that women have an important social role to play in the development of the country, and that it need not be in conflict with the Islamic values.

General Ziaul Haq, during his regime, introduced certain measures as part of his Islamicization programme which caused considerable debate about the rights of women in Islam (see, for example, Carrol 1982; Mumtaz and Shaheed 1987; Mehdi 1994). My objective is to focus on the polemical literature in which the issues relating to women's rights in the context of martial law ordinances were examined. *Purdah and Polygamy* by Mazhar ul Haq Khan (1972) is the one exception as a book which pre-dates the martial law period but is highly relevant to the subject under consideration. Most of the other critical contributions consist of articles and commentaries which were published in the English language newspapers during that period, especially *The Pakistan Times*. These writings are, of course, accessible only to a small educated minority in the country and it is perhaps for this reason that they were tolerated by the government and the ulama. Nevertheless, this literature represents a significant challenge to the conventional views of the ulama. It is also interesting to note that no comparable discussions took place in the Urdu press in the period under consideration.

The essential theme of this chapter is that the moral, religious, and social pronouncements of the Qur'an have a social-historical context. The interpretation of the Qur'anic law, then, must consist of a movement from the present situation to the Qur'anic times and then back to the present. This task has been made easier by the recent work of Riffat Hassan (1987), Fatima Mernissi (1992), and Leila Ahmed (1992). These three authors in their respective approaches to the question of women in Islam have carefully and thoroughly examined the historical roots of the traditional views of the ulama on the subject. The literature that I propose to review below did not have the benefit of these contributions.

Purda, and the Qur'an

Purda literally means a veil or a curtain, but according to the traditional view it is a code of conduct for Muslim women. This view is succinctly expressed by Abul A'la Maudoodi who has written a number of articles and commentaries on this question. (References in this chapter are from his *Purdah*, 1967). Starting from puberty, according to Maudoodi, a woman must observe certain rules of behaviour both inside and outside the house. The indoor restrictions would prohibit admittance of any male other than from the prescribed list of close relatives. The outdoor restrictions would require her to cover herself completely except for the upper part of the face. She must dress modestly and use a veil. There is no serious discussion in Maudoodi's writings, or of other ulama, concerning the possible use of *khimar* (a wimple supplemented by a loose-fitting dress) that is apparently approved by the religious right in some Middle Eastern countries as an 'Islamic' dress. For the traditionalist ulama of Pakistan, women will not participate in the labour force in an ideal Islamic society. Therefore, the *burqa* (a billowing white cotton cloth...allowing vision through netting over the eyeholes—Papanek 1973: 295), or *chadar* (a sheet to wrap the body and face except for the eyes) will suffice for their limited excursions outside the house which in any case will have to be in the company of chaperons.

The Qur'anic verses which are invoked in support of *purda* are 24:30–31; 33:32–3 and 59. The first two verses ask the believers to lower their gaze and be modest, and (for women) to display only those parts of their adornments that are necessary, and to draw their veils over their bosoms. In verses 33:32–3, the wives of the Prophet are addressed and they are reminded that they are not like other women and, therefore, they should stay at home and not display their finery as in the pagan customs. The position of the modernists concerning these verses is that no specific dress is being prescribed for women, and that the purpose of the Qur'an is to establish ethical norms by giving directions with regard to the pre-Islamic practices. The problem, then, lies with the Islamic jurisprudence which developed in its formative period under the influence of medieval values. And, there are additional factors that have played their role in the evolution of the Muslim view of women in the Indian subcontinent.

In a carefully argued paper, 'Images of Women in the Social and Cultural life', Anis Mirza (1984), says that the present custom of *purda* has its roots in the confluence of the two cultures, Hinduism and Islam. The system seems to have grown with the Huns, and later with Rajputs. The ruling class women among the Huns were usually heavily adorned with jewelry and long robes, and were not allowed to mix with the indigenous masses. Among the Rajputs, segregation and separate living enclosures for women became the pattern. 'This separateness generated a romantic imagery of the female—sweet, feminine, helpless, lovelorn, and forlorn—which we have seen in the Mughal-Rajput miniature paintings of the Pahari School. In our time, Abdur Rahman Chughtai immortalized the hazel-eyed oriental women...'(ibid). Mirza suggests that the Mughals and the Arabs, as they came later to the scene, introduced segregation and *purda* in the upper classes and with time it became a middle class symbol in the cities, and a protective shroud against the gazing eyes of the strangers (ibid).

Mazhar ul Haq Khan focuses on the Arab customs as they developed in the context of the harem and the ruling elite of the society. *Purda* spread from the upper classes to the community at large and it was proclaimed as an Islamic institution by the Abbasid ruler Al-Qadir AD 991–1031 (1972: 33; also Syed Ameer Ali 1927: 455ff). The classical jurists were the product of their times and could not but have been influenced by this phenomenon. It was in such a social atmosphere that the medieval Muslims, both the ulama and others, misinterpreted the Qur'anic injunctions concerning the status of women. 'Not only it (the *purda* system and its ideology) disregarded the very spirit of Islam which proclaims woman to be a free and equal personality, but also denied that she has any will or personality of her own: she is only pudentality incarnate' (Khan, ibid: 34). Mazhar ul Haq notes with surprise, therefore, that for Abul A'la Maudoodi harem was 'the strongest fortress for the Islamic civilization which was built for the reasons that, if ever suffered a reverse, it may then take refuge in it' (Khan: 34).

The sequestration of women and the use of *purda* are closely related in the Muslim culture of Pakistan. Women can be kept, however, in a separate world from men without resorting to the strict sartorial requirements for them. By using a form of segregation, many societies in Asia and the Pacific manage to promote virtues of chastity, modesty, and obedience for women. But the traditionalist ulama use the Western model to claim that absence of *purda* leads to sexual anarchy. 'Look at those who don't hide their women at all', says Israr Ahmed who has made headlines in the Pakistan press from time to time with his controversial views. And, 'do you know the ratio of rape and *zina* (adultery) in the West?' This obviously refers to the mixing of sexes, because 'women hold an attraction for men'. But Israr Ahmed contradicts himself in the next sentence when he suggests that 'their (women's) presence before men will only decrease that attraction' (Jafri 1986: 132; also on Israr Ahmed's views see Mumtaz and Shaheed 1987: 83ff). The entire burden of maintaining sexual order, then, falls on women because Israr Ahmed, like other ulama, has no advice for men in this regard (e.g. Qur'an 24:30–31). This single-minded attitude can only be explained with reference to what Fatima Mernissi regards as the main assumption about women in the Islamic system: that she is a source of *fitna* (a word of many meanings, a source of trouble in this context), and that she is endowed with a fatal attraction which erodes men's will to resist her (1975: 1–14). Perhaps the sociological factors such as *gherat* (modesty, shame), *izzat* (honour), and a strong commitment to kinship and patrilineal links, as emphasized by Mazhar ul Haq have further contributed to this attitude of men towards women. What is then paraded as an Islamic virtue is in fact rooted in the social fabric of a traditional society.

How close is the reality of observance of *purda* to the traditionalists' model? The National Impact Survey conducted in 1968–69 showed that 82 per cent of women in urban areas and 47 per cent in rural areas either wore a *burqa* or a *chadar*. A Lahore study for 1982 indicated that the proportion of *burqa*-using urban women was 87 in that year (Shah 1986: 343–7). This coincides with the policies of Ziaul Haq to introduce 'Islamic' dress for women starting in 1980, requiring all government women employees to use a chadar over whatever they may be wearing. There is no legally defined dress for women, but the force of custom is clearly in favour of *shalwar qameez* (a long shirt over baggy trousers), and the right-wing opinion considers use of *sari* as un-Islamic. It is difficult to gauge the psychological impact of the government directive. During the sixties and the seventies, the plain all-covering cloak had been replaced by the two-part *burqa* made of rayon or silk, and the *dupatta* (a long scarf covering the head or, draped over shoulders) and had become attractive and diaphanous (Papanek 1973: 296). It seems, however, that the degrees of *purda* observed by women when they were not playing an official or public role varied and were linked to class and subculture during the eighties, and this seems to be the continuing trend. *Purda* is, nevertheless, an attitude of mind and a mode of behaviour and the main goal of General Ziaul Haq regime was to promote these attributes in women.

The Family and the Qur'an

The traditionalists believe that it is necessary for women to devote their entire energies to the home for the preservation of family life. Character formation begins in infancy within the family. Abul A'la Maudoodi sums up the position of the traditionalists as follows (1967: 193ff):

(1) It is the man's responsibility to earn a living for the family, while the woman must make domestic life a paradise of peace and joy—she must therefore receive the best possible education and training in order to perform her duties.

(2) Women are inferior to men: 'You cannot produce a single women of the calibre of Ibn Sina, a Kant, a Hegel, an Umar Khayyam, a Shakespeare, an Alexander, a Napolean, a Salahuddin, a Nizam ul Mulk or a Bismarck (p. 193).'

(3) Women are unable to perform most of the outdoor work, not just the heavy physical activity, but also the economic, political, and administrative duties. She is a tragic being, with all those bodily and reproductive functions to perform; the domestic role is ordained for her by nature. 'Biology, Anatomy, Physiology, Psychology and all the branches of Sociology prescribe this division (of labour)' (quoted by Mazhar ul Haq Khan 1972: 199).

Mazhar ul Haq Khan examines Maudoodi's arguments in detail and suggests that these arguments have no basis in Islam and cannot be sustained under any serious social analysis. What is important about Maudoodi's position is its pretence about its legitimacy as derived from the Qur'an. 'The tragedy of woman is not biological, it is sociological and ideological' (p. 209). Maudoodi's views are important for another reason. The Jama'at-e-Islami under his leadership forged an alliance with General Ziaul Haq during the early period of his rule for establishing the 'Islamic Order' through martial law ordinances.

Mazhar ul Haq Khan is one of the few Pakistani writers who has critically examined the life of a woman in what he calls the *purda* family. His observations relate to the sixties and the seventies, but there is no reason to believe that the situation had changed for the better under the Ziaul Haq regime. The *purda* family is patriarchal, the woman as wife has no intimate relations with her husband whom she treats with respect as the source of authority in the house. As mother, she raises her children under a heavy dose of 'don't' and threats; in general she has no idea how to inculcate discipline in the child concerning feeding, sleeping, and toilet; she has little knowledge about diet, proteins, and calories. As a daughter, she learns early on that her situation in life requires her to defer completely to her husband and other men of the household, depending upon the pecking order, and of course to the mother-in-law. 'Living in a social vacuum, the *purda* girl has little or no opportunity to learn the habits and methods of social behaviour and adjustment towards other people' (p. 99). By the time she reaches the age of 10 or 12, the woman as daughter has already developed deep-seated fears of the outside world of men. The restrictive atmosphere of life in the segregated home, along with the psychological distance which the *purda* girl feels from her father and brothers, 'coupled with the taunts of inferiority and direct and indirect prohibitions against a more active, vigorous and ambitious life produce definite effects on the mind and character of the *purda* girl' (p. 89). For her the role model of her mother is a harassed woman, facing constant tensions in the family, financial worries, and personal anxieties about the husband's possible outside escapades (p. 90).

Nasra M. Shah has recently collected statistical information about Pakistani women. 'From the meagre data available,' she says, '...we know that the husband's approval (or disapproval) is an important factor in determining whether the wife will indulge in a certain kind of behaviour or not' (Shah 1986: 348). However, she is likely to take full advantage of any loopholes in the family life to exercise her freedom, according to Gulnaz Chaudhry (1987). She would fudge food prices to allow herself some financial manoeuvrability; she would surreptitiously reach at the husband's safe or his pocket. Her manipulative powers can extend to important matters such as arranging for a potential husband for the daughter.

In general, the women in Pakistan seem to be able to negotiate roles for themselves that define their relations with their husbands, like their counterparts in the Middle East, as pointed out in an ethnographic study of that region (Nelson 1974). Although no reliable information is available on the subject with respect to Pakistan, casual observation seems to suggest that like Middle Eastern women Pakistani women do maintain an intricate network of relationships with other members of the same sex. This relationship, however, does not reach much beyond their private (i.e. household) sphere. In fact, the scope for a woman's freedom of action in the negotiated order of the family (e.g., networking, information broker, etc.) appears to be quite limited. Women are induced to defensive strategies in the name of family honour and, owing to their dependent status, these strategies are influenced by a hierarchy of age and of relations with dominant males. The gender inequities persist, therefore, because the conflicts of interest are normally not given to open struggle. In this manner, the *purda* family becomes durable and stable. A majority of women cannot envisage an alternative life style, and some of them might even feel threatened by attacks on this mode of family life.

There is a variety of social, economic, and political obstacles which would have to be overcome before the existing pattern of *purda* life can be changed. The religious factor, however, is of paramount importance. The traditionalists invoke several verses of the Qur'an in favour of keeping, and even strengthening, the status quo. There are three main aspects involved in this issue: marriage, interspousal relations, and inheritance. These are discussed below in this order.

(1) Marriage: According to the Qur'an, marriage is a most solemn affair; it is a contract, a firm agreement (verse 4:21). Men are advised to marry when they can afford it and to keep themselves 'chaste until Allah provides them with such means' (verse 24:33). The basis of marriage is love and kindness (verse 30:21). These religious prescriptions about marriage are universally endorsed by Muslims. The Qur'anic law and practice, however, begin to diverge when it comes to matters such as divorce and wife's maintenance. The Qur'an does not accept divorce as a first resort and it recommends arbitration so that an attempt may be made to resolve the conflict (verse 4:35). When the final separation does take place, the husband is required to make an honourable provision for the divorced woman (verse 2:241). This is in addition to *mehr* that the bridegroom agrees to pay the prospective bride in accordance with the Islamic law. In practice, however, the husband may divorce his wife instantly by pronouncing his decision three times consecutively. This method of separation—the 'innovational' divorce—seems to have the approval of the vast majority of the traditionalist ulama. Rafiullah Shehab in his discussion of this custom suggests that the source of confusion about the legal status of this method of divorce in Islam goes back perhaps to the Second Caliph of Islam, Umar, who is reported to have recognized this divorce only to make the husband face the consequences of his decision: he could not remarry the woman without having her gone through another marriage (1986: 82). When the Caliph discovered that third-party fake marriages (*halalah*) were being used to get around his ruling he relented. 'It must be borne in mind that Hazrat Umar's decision was the result of the exigencies of the situation and *talaq al-Sunnah* (i.e., the Qur'anic system of divorce) continued to be considered the only proper Islamic way of divorce' (p. 83).

The question of maintenance allowance for the divorced wife has never been seriously discussed in Pakistan. It is widely assumed that apart from *mehr*, if it has already not been paid, the husband owes nothing to his divorced wife. Shehab argues that according to the principles of the Hanafi school of jurisprudence, which is used by a majority of Muslims in the country, the husband should maintain his wife in a proper manner and that she deserves her maintenance allowance not only as a wife but also after divorce. In this context, he refers to the Shah Bano case according to which the appellant won her claim at the Supreme Court of India, only to be thwarted by the political process of the country under pressure from the traditionalist ulama (pp. 219–22).

The Qur'anic message about marriage and divorce is addressed to the believers using the masculine gender, but its ethical thrust is quite clear, according to the modernist writers. A marriage contract may be drawn, for example, to protect the interests of the wife which would include delegated power of divorce, *talaq-e-tafwid,* (Ahmed 1984; his article is based on a speech delivered by the then Chief Justice of the Lahore High Court, Dr Javed Iqbal to the International Women's Club in that city). Another course of action that is available to women is what is called *khula* which is incorporated in the (Indian) Dissolution of Muslim Marriage Act of 1939 as applied to Pakistan, though under this act the wife can be required to forgo some of the rights and benefits received from the husband. There is, therefore, a clear distinction between the right of divorce by husband (*talaq*) and the right of the wife (*khula*—to forgo some benefits in exchange for divorce). According to Shehab, the woman's right to *khula* should not require consent of the court except when the amount of compensation involved in the matter is in dispute (p. 18).

Whether a man can marry more than one wife according to the Qur'an depends on how verses 4:2–3 as well as 4:127–9 are interpreted. These verses were revealed to deal with the situation that arose following the battle of Uhud when a large number of widows and orphans had been left as a result of heavy casualties suffered by men in this battle. The verses do not enjoin polygamy and they do not even permit it unconditionally. The polygamous man must do justice as between his wives (verse 4:3), but he does not have it in his power to fulfil this responsibility, however, much he may wish to do so (verse 4:129). This apparent contradiction between the verses was resolved by the early jurists, says Fazlur Rahman, by giving legal status to the permission for four wives but reducing the prescription of justice between wives to a private recommendation to the polygamous husband (Rahman 1983). He elaborates his point further with reference to al-Tabari, a classical jurist who gave five different interpretations of these verses, all of which were speculative, none fitting the Qur'anic passages. 'If such a practical ordinance is so speculatively interpreted by the 3rd/9th century this should warn us that there is something wrong or rather there is some fundamental dislocation between what the Qur'an is saying and the practice of the community' (ibid). Mazhar ul Haq Khan argues that the practice of the community has deep roots in the social history of Islam, particularly with reference to the harem system which affected the life and character of Muslims in a degenerative manner (Khan, op. cit., p. 37).

(2) Interspousal Relations: The Qur'an treats men and women equally— '...men who believe and women who believe...', and it reminds men that women have the same human status as themselves (3:195). This is a radical message to the tribal society in which the birth of a daughter was never welcome. Now we live in an era in which the relations between men and women have been redefined. To combat the modern trends towards equality between the sexes, the traditionalists invoke the Qur'anic verses 33:32 and 33: '...and stay in your houses...'. These

verses, however, are addressed to the Prophet's wives—
'you are not like any other women'. For Asghar Butt, the
position of the traditionalists is untenable on this issue,
because it is not the purpose of the Qur'an to confine
women to their homes except under special circumstances
such as being guilty of an immoral act, 4:19 (Butt 1982).
The traditionalists, however, try to reinforce their
arguments with reference to verse 4:34. According to the
popular translation of the verse, men are in charge of
women as God has made one of them (i.e. men) superior
to the other (i.e. women). But in verse 9:17 men and
women are declared as being protectors of each other.
Mazhar ul Haq Khan is of the view that the source of
misunderstanding about the intention of the Qur'an is the
Arabic word *qavvamoon* which, if properly translated makes
men maintainers, not in charge of women. '...the power of
maintenance of the husband is intended by the Qur'an as a
moral and a sublimatory power to devote his superior
strength to productive labour, to assist in the dynamic
development and fulfilment of his wife and children and
not act as a restraint on them' (Khan, op. cit., p. 149).
Similarly, the statement in the verse that 'Good women are
...obedient...' surely must refer to obedience to God. Also
in verse 2:228, it is in the context of the constraint imposed
on men concerning their right to divorce women during
the menstruation period that the Qur'an declares that
women have rights similar to those which the husbands
have against their wives, but men are a degree above them.
Again it has been suggested that the degree of superiority
of men refers to their power of maintenance as mentioned
in verse 4:34.

Fazlur Rahman argues that this verse cannot be separated
from the socio-historical circumstances of the Prophet's
time. The economic functions on the basis of which the
gender inequality evolved are not unchangeable, and
'...given necessary time, women will also acquire the same
experiences and wisdom that men have accumulated over

the ages.' However, '...whether women should ask for or be allowed to do all or any jobs that men are doing, I am not at all sure of (Rehman 1983).

There remains, nevertheless, a strong presumption of inequality between men and women. Tahira Maryam (1987) underlines this point with reference to the question of punishment for the misbehaviour of a wife. According to verse 4:34, the rebellious women are to be admonished, banished to bed and scourged. In verse 4:15, if they are guilty of lewdness, they are to be confined to the house until death takes them or God appoints for them a way (i.e. a court decision as interpreted by most translators of the Qur'an). In verse 4:16 a slight punishment is prescribed when both men and women are guilty of an indecent act. Shehab points out that these verses are not addressed to husband and wife; they relate to society's responsibilities to its citizens. Also, the language of the Qur'an needs to be carefully noted. In verse 4:16, the Arabic word *fazoohuma* has been used which literally means 'to beat' but it has been rendered as a 'slight punishment' by most translators of the Qur'an. In verse 4:34, on the other hand, the word *zaraba* is usually translated as 'to beat' whereas in the legal context it means 'to prevent' (Shehab, op. cit., p. 117).

(3) Inheritance: Islam was the first among world civilizations to recognize the property rights of women. Their share in inheritance was defined by the Qur'an differently for different situations. No accurate data are available to show whether the Qur'anic prescription is scrupulously followed. From time to time, however, cases are reported in which daughters are deprived of their rights to property by means of a variety of subterfuges as reported by the *Herald* (Karachi, September 1985). There is also a general belief that a woman's share is half that of man, according to the Qur'an. The Muslim modernists contend that in the context of the present-day society all children should receive equal shares irrespective of their sex. The

original inheritance shares were a function of their actual roles in the traditional society. 'With social change, however, changes in shares must follow, since in a detribalized society functions undergo radical changes', says Fazlur Rahman (op. cit., 1983). This point is further emphasized by Shehab in his discussion of verse 4:11 as follows: 'In this verse different shares of women have been fixed in three different cases of inheritance. In the first case, the share of a daughter has been fixed as half that of a son....In the second case, the share of both mother and father has been fixed as one-sixth. Here the woman gets share equal to that of the man. In the third case while the share of father remains one-sixth, the share of mother has been doubled as one-third of the whole property' (op. cit., pp. 215–16).

The question concerning the Islamic laws of inheritance has already been discussed in Chapter 5 above. It would be useful, however, to make a brief reference to the laws of Pakistan which were introduced to protect the rights of women, prior to the martial law of General Ziaul Haq. In the area of direct legislation concerning women, only two measures are worth noting: The Muslim Family Laws Ordinance of 1961, and the Dowry and Bridal Gifts (Restrictions) Act of 1976. The former is honoured more in breach than observance, and the latter seems to have created unfavourable results for women, contrary to its intention. With regard to constitutional guarantees, the 1973 Constitution was more strongly supportive of women's rights than the previous constitutions.

The 1973 Constitution envisaged a parliamentary system based on universal adult franchise. It ensured full participation of women in all walks of life, and it declared against discrimination on the basis of sex or creed. It made provision for their representation in the political process of the country: it reserved one seat in the Council of Islamic Ideology, and seats in provincial and national assemblies to be elected indirectly and virtually by all-male constituencies. The text of the Constitution is inconsistent in many respects and would require suitable elaborations.

The 1976 Act was passed by the government of Z.A. Bhutto towards the very end of its term. Little attention was given to it by the regime of Ziaul Haq and not much real progress has been made since his time. The custom of dowry—the payments and gifts by the bride's family to the bridegroom and his family and not to be confused with *mehr* —is alien to the Islamic culture, but it continues to be an important part of marriage ceremonies, like many other selective features of the Indo-Muslim style of life of Pakistanis. This is where the Act comes into play and begins to serve as a hindrance to the rights of women when they seek recovery of assets after divorce. Men manage to take refuge behind the limits imposed by the Act, though courts seem to have leaned on the side of the women in cases where the matter was brought to their attention.

How the Family Laws Ordinance came into being is well known and need not be repeated here. The Ordinance does not incorporate all the recommendations of the Commission on Marriage and Family Laws, 1965, concerning legal protection for married and divorced women (Smith 1971: 71–9). The commission consisted of members representing various shades of opinion in the country. Maulana Ihteshamul Haq, a traditionalist *alim* who represented the orthodox constituency, underlines the dilemma facing the Islamic Pakistan through his dissenting note to the report of the Commission (ibid. p. 76). What exactly is the Muslim law, and who has the right to pronounce authoritative interpretation of this law? The ulama alone are competent to deal with any matters relating to the sharia, according to the Maulana, which is the legacy of opinions and verdicts of the classical jurists. '...in spite of their blatant departure from the views of the Muslim commentators and jurists, no member of the Commission could take the place of Fakhruddin Razi or Abu Hanifa' (ibid.).

The main features of the Ordinance include the guarantee of inheritance by orphans of pre-deceased children, registration of marriages, notification of intention of divorce to an appropriate local official, reconciliation proceedings prior to divorce, and permission of the arbitration council for taking another wife by a man and involving consent of the existing wife or wives (Mahmood 1986: 1–75 and 105–179). The Ordinance was hailed by the progressive elements as a remarkable achievement. It was, however, a first step and a very modest step in the right direction. In its attempt to control polygamy, it may have put an extraordinary burden on the existing wife, especially a middle-aged woman. But there was at least the presumption against unfettered multiple marriages. The requirement of the registration of the ceremony allowed for the possibility of negotiating a favourable contract for the bride whose minimum age was raised to 16 years.

The Constitutions of 1962 and 1973 protected the Ordinance against judicial challenge. The orthodox opinion, however, has been consistently against the Ordinance, with the exception of Maudoodi whose position concerning polygamy, innovational divorce, and child marriages as expounded in his *Huququl Zaujain* (1943) was similar to what was later on incorporated in the Ordinance, but who joined the chorus against the Ordinance in 1961, and his views are included in the *Studies in the Family Laws of Islam*, published by Chirag-e-Rah Publications in that year. It is also worth noting that Tanzilur-Rahman, who had been an adviser of General Ziaul Haq in his capacity as a member and chairman of the Council of Islamic Ideology, and later served as Chief Justice of the Federal Shariat Court, had prepared a list of Islamic laws under the aegis of the Islamic Research Institute in 1971 (during the Z.A. Bhutto regime). The innovational divorce as well as the *halalah* custom were included in this list as proper Islamic institutions (Shehab, op. cit., pp. 85–6).

The future of the Ordinance is quite uncertain. One of its main provisions, Section 7, requiring the man to notify the local official of his pronouncement of divorce, has been declared invalid by a court. Another court has recently announced that Section 6 of the Ordinance concerning restrictions on polygamy is repugnant to Islam. These judicial opinions create uncertainty about the law. The enforcement of the Sharia Act passed during the period of Nawaz Sharif as Prime Minister in 1991 is bound to lead to further legal challenges of the Ordinance. And the policy of deliberate indifference towards Islamicization of Ziaul Haq pursued by the government of Benazir Bhutto during her first as well as the second opportunity as prime minister has in fact weakened the position of the modernists in the country.

Women and Islamicization of Laws

The Hudood Laws of 1979 have been a focus of controversy in the country. The amendments to the Law of Evidence, 1984 have similarly been received with considerable reservations, and the question of *Qisas* and *Diyat* underlines the bias against equality of women by the traditionalist ulama. These measures were an attempt to establish an Islamic atmosphere in the country by applying the medieval classical interpretations of Islamic laws to the country. The recommendations for these measures originated with the Council of Islamic Ideology that was reconstituted by General Ziaul Haq under the provisions of the 1973 Constitution to represent the fundamentalist viewpoint on Islam.

The Hudood Laws is a collective term for four ordinances concerning enforcement of prohibition of drinking, and punishments for adultery, slander, and theft. It is the second ordinance—Offense of *Zina*: Enforcement of Hudood Ordinance, 1979—that is of direct relevance for discussion. The purpose of the ordinance is to amend the Indian Penal Code of 1898 in order to bring it in conformity with the classical Islamic law. For *zina* (adultery, fornication, and prostitution) the maximum punishment when the required evidence (voluntary confession or testimony of four upright Muslim males) for the *hadd* (the limit as defined in the Qur'an and Sunna) is available is death by stoning. With any other type of evidence, the crime is punishable by *tazir* (lesser than *hadd*) and includes lashes and imprisonment. The law is essentially the same for *zina-bil-jabr* (rape) as for *zina* except that the punishment for this crime when it is considered under *tazir* is greater than for *zina* (Patel 1986: 41–51; Mumtaz and Shaheed: 100–105)

There has been an outrage concerning this ordinance among the modernist Pakistanis and especially among the women's groups in the country. Sad tales of women caught in the web of its archaic provisions are often reported in the press. It has been suggested, however, that the implementation of the Hudood Ordinance has had only a marginal impact on Pakistan's criminal law system, though it may have been skewed against the lower income groups in the country. Nevertheless, the main point about the ordinance is its political and psychological impact. It represents a political victory for the traditionalist ulama, at least in the short run. It has created a psychological environment that would appeal to the primitive instinct of men with its vague definitions and adultery and rape, its requirement for testimony of male witnesses and its provision for lashes and stoning to death.

The new Law of Evidence is another example in which the medieval jurisprudence is being applied to modern times. Unlike the Hudood Ordinance, a Qur'anic verse (2:282) is directly linked with this issue. Shehab challenges the views of the ulama and concludes: 'This verse does not equate evidence of two women...to that of one man...only one women has to give evidence concerning a financial contract...The function of the other accompanying woman is to save the witnessing woman from any confusion or embarrassment' (Shehab 1986: 187–8). Fazlur Rahman says that this requirement relates to the socio-historical context of the Qur'anic period and that when circumstances change so that women not only get education equal to men, but also become conversant with business and finance then this stipulation of the Qur'an becomes unnecessary (Rahman 1983).

The issue of *qisas* and *diyat* which the traditionalist ulama regard as an integral part of Islamicization represents a serious discrimination against women in the eyes of law. In the case of *diyat* (blood money) the compensation for the female victim of the crime would be half that of male, and in the case of *qisas* (retaliation) testimony of two Muslim male witnesses would be necessary (Patel: 147–8). Shehab suggests that these two proposals have no basis in Islam. '...if the proposed rate of *diyat* of women is made legal, then as its corollary, it will imply that the punishment for the *qisas* should also be reduced to one-half' (pp. 187–8).

Concluding Remarks

It is clear from the above discussion that the question concerning the rights of women has been linked with the political process of the country. It was always understood that Islamic values would play an important role in Pakistan. What kind of Islam and according to whose interpretation—the modernists or the traditionalists—was the main issue but it was always ignored. The politicians and the ulama have been playing a game in which the former seek their support for their legitimacy and the latter can prey upon their susceptibilities in the name of the perceived 'revolt' of Islam. The old jurisprudence in its pristine glory cannot, however, withstand the stresses and strains of modern times. To make people aware of this fact requires a massive educational enterprise.

Recently a small book in Urdu was published by Ghulam Akbar Malik called *Aurat ka Muqaddama: Islam ki Adalat mein* (1991), broadly translated as ' The case of woman in the court of Islam'. The book deals with the historical roots of modern debate on the status of women in Islam. He examines the old Judeo-Christian views on creation, and he notes that even though these views have now been discarded in the West, they continue to have a strong hold on Muslim psyche. The story of Adam and Eve is in clear contradiction to the Qur'anic approach to creation.

Mr Mailk points out with reference to the Qur'anic verse 4:34 (referring to men as maintainers of women) cannot be invoked against women, because there is no general agreement about the context of this verse, and that it must be interpreted in light of the Qur'anic message that men and women are equal. As for the literature dealing with the traditions of the Prophet, he illustrates the problem with reference to a saying ascribed to the Prophet that a nation led by a woman would never prosper. He explains that it refers to a particular situation then prevailing in Persia. Similarly, he expands on his theme on other issues, arguing that the modern context of the old juristic pronouncements about women need to be carefully examined. This task has been done thoroughly by writers like Fatima Mernissi. The fact that this approach to the issue has been adopted by a local Urdu writer is very encouraging.

NOTE

1. This chapter is a revised version of my article on 'Women and Islam in Pakistan', published in the *Middle Eastern Studies* 26: 4, 1990.

CHAPTER 8

State and Religion

In this chapter, I propose to focus on the fulcrum of my argument, the relation between state and religion. This relationship provides a framework for the economic issues I have discussed in this book and of course it affects all aspects of life in the country. The main points I have already made are worth repeating. Jinnah envisaged Pakistan to be a secular democratic state, a Muslim state in which the people would be able to shape their lives without the fear of Hindu domination. Nevertheless, he invoked religion in his appeal for unity and in his statements concerning the future structure of the economy of Pakistan. From Liaquat Ali Khan to Z. A. Bhutto, emphasis on Islam to legitimize the role of the political leadership became increasingly evident and the country became the Islamic Republic of Pakistan.

The leaders of the country during this period remained predominantly secular in their outlook. They seemed to look to the Islamic modernists to establish a bridge between their Western style constitutional approach to the state and Islamic law. In the realm of economic policy, it was expected that new interpretations of Islamic injunctions would be established, and that these interpretations would resolve any real or apparent conflict between the structure of the modern economy in the framework of the emerging globalization and Islamic values. No concerted effort was made, however, to give the necessary support to the Islamic modernists. There was no political commitment to an explicit goal in this regard, only an incrementalist policy which was followed to avoid direct conflict with the traditional ulama. This phase of political zigzagging was brought to an end by General Ziaul Haq. It was also the period in which, as already pointed out in this book, there was emergence of Islamic economics in Pakistan and other countries of the Muslim world.

Islamic Economics and Islamic Modernism

Islamic economics claims to deal with the issues relating to economic principles and policies suitable for an Islamic state. It was partly born out of doctoral dissertations on Islamic finance and banking, but mainly it was the product of series of books, pamphlets, and articles written on the subject. Its growth reached its peak during the seventies. Such a flow of literature with a concerted focus on a specific subject, and in a short span of time, could not have resulted from a spontaneous spurt of contributions under this heading. The general assumption is that petro-dollars provided the necessary financial support, and there was timely patronage from political regimes such as that of General Ziaul Haq.

I have emphasized throughout this book that the main pillars of Islamic economics—the abolition of *riba*, the establishment of *zakat* and *ushr*, and implementation of the laws of inheritance—are based entirely on the interpretations of the traditional ulama concerning these injunctions. The literature on interest-free banking, for example, is based on the assumption that the Qur'anic *riba* includes interest as used in modern times. Similarly, *zakat*, *ushr* and the laws of inheritance are defined in accordance with the views of the ulama. The economic structure of an Islamic state, according to the Islamic economists, would necessarily be based on the revival of the institutional framework of the medieval period, which is the cherished objective of the traditionalist ulama and their political supporters.

Confusion of Ideology

General Ziaul Haq's evangelical pursuit of Islamicization undermined the progressive elements in the country. As discussed in Chapter 1, the transplantation of the medieval Islamic institutions pursued by him was carefully planned and was highly selective from the point of view of maximizing legitimacy of his regime. Interest-free banking, Hudood Ordinances, *zakat* and *ushr*, as well as establishment of the *Majlis-e-Shoora* on the basis of elections in which political parties were not permitted to campaign were targets which were to enhance his power. The basic framework of Pakistan, however, remained secular, as it had been since August 1947. The differentiated bureaucracy, the Western-style army and his own rank in it, the Senate, being the upper house of the parliamentary structure, and the financial system of the state at all three levels of government, were maintained. An important consequence of his rule was the growth of sectarianism in the country.

Pakistan was to be an ideological state under his regime with ideology defined by him and his collaborators among the traditional ulama and professional groups. The rewriting of textbooks was accelerated to underline this ideology, emphasizing the link of the idea of Pakistan with the birth of Islam on the Arabian peninsula, and claiming that Pakistan was not a geographical entity but an ideology which reflected a unique civilization and culture (Jalal 1995, Aziz 1993). From history to Islamic economics was an easy step forward. In the area of science, the Islamic view of the solar system and of the physical laws of nature was promoted (Hoodbhoy 1991).

In some respects, the process which started with the Objectives Resolution reached its climax under Ziaul Haq. Liaquat Ali Khan presumably assumed that he could make a controlled use of religion through his constitutional approach by enunciating Directive Principles of State Policy but leaving the question of details for the government to decide. The Resolution was used as a preamble in later constitutions and it was made substantive part of the 1973 Constitution by an amendment through a presidential order issued by Ziaul Haq in 1985. The effects of this amendment on other provisions of the constitution are not clear and the Supreme Court seems not to have accepted its place overriding other constitutional principles such as sanctity of contract even when payment of interest is involved.

The period since Ziaul Haq continues with the confusion of ideology. The two major political parties in the country, the Muslim League and the People's Party, have been contributing to this confusion in their own respective ways. For the former, it is important to endorse Ziaul Haq, at least rhetorically, as the great saviour of Islam. For the latter, a deliberate indifference to his legacy has been the best approach for political survival.

Islamic Modernism in Retreat

The following phrase in the Objectives Resolution—'the Muslims shall be enabled to order their lives...in accordance with...Islam...'—is a challenge which requires a reinterpretation and reconstruction of religious thought in Islam in the context of modern times. Many of the Qur'anic laws are of deductive nature, but the inductive approach towards establishing rules is predominant in the Qur'an, and it was of the essence of the Prophetic mission. There has of course been a fundamental change in the social fabric from the days of the Prophet (PBUH). The laws of jurisprudence are man-made and were established mainly by the four schools of jurisprudence in light of the demands of the prevailing social structure. The Muslim modernists have made an effort to bridge this gap. Syed Ahmad Khan made a personal attempt to interpret Islam and to establish its compatibility with reason and science. Syed Ameer Ali was a social modernist who argued that it was necessary to distinguish between moral precepts and specific legal prescriptions of the Qur'an, pointing to slavery as an example which was legally permitted but with a moral plea to free slaves (1939). Sir Hamilton Gibb accuses Muslim modernists (including Iqbal) of subjective selectivity in order to promote their own interpretation of Islam (1947). As Fazlur Rahman says, these charges are correct, to some extent, against a classical modernist like Syed Ameer Ali. Nevertheless, whatever elements in their history the modernists praise and emphasize they are not so much portraying the past as indirectly pointing to the future (1966: 235–6).

Iqbal is highly relevant for my argument, however. In Chapter 1, I referred to Iqbal's concept of Islamic law. His total message in his *Reconstruction of Religious Thought* as well as his poetry is very complex; he is arguing for Faith and is suspicious of reason. His stature by virtue of his message was such that he was declared a spiritual founder of Pakistan. There has been use and abuse of his poetry, but his *Reconstruction* has been completely ignored in the elite circles of Pakistan. It has remained 'a purely personal statement of the Islamic Faith and has not so far been able to function as a datum-line from which further developments could take place' (Rahman 1966: 226).

Iqbal explains the dynamics of the Islamic law with reference to the Qur'an and the traditions of the Prophet. In his discussion of *ijma*, the third source of Islamic law, he notes that the modern legislative assembly is the only suitable vehicle for its use (p. 174). He was not in favour of the 'Persian Constitution' which provided for a separate ecclesiastical committee of ulama to supervise the legislative activity of the Mejlis. He agreed, however, that the ulama should have an important role to play in the formation of law but only as a vital part of the legislative assembly helping and guiding free discussion on questions relating to law (p. 176).

The Pakistan constitution in its Islamic provisions includes the establishment of a Council of Islamic Ideology which is required to report its findings to the legislative assembly. This arrangement might appear to be following a middle ground between the Persian Constitution and Iqbal's recommendation. In reality, the Council has been acting like a semi-ecclesiastical body. During the period of Ayub Khan, there was serious tension between its approach to Islamic injunctions and that of the Islamic Research Institute. With General Ziaul Haq it became a conduit for presidential orders and ordinances for his Islamicization policy.

The role of the ulama as elected members of the legislature would be very different, with their responsibilities to their constituencies which elected them and to the country as a whole. There is supposed to be no 'church' in Islam, at least in the Sunni tradition. The ulama, however, seem to enjoy a position high enough to act like ecclesiastical leaders. For Ummayid and Abbasid caliphs, Iqbal suggests, it was a safer arrangement to invest the power of *ijtehad* in individual mujtahids rather than forming a permanent assembly which might become too powerful for them (p. 173).

In view of their highly specialized knowledge about Islam, it is important that the ulama occupy a distinct place in the Islamic community. The political role of this elite group, however, as the instrument for implementing religious and legal precepts seems to be exaggerated. There is no manifest decline in this establishment which could be associated with the diminution of the scope of the sharia, a relation Schacht seems to suggest (1953: 524–9). The fall of the caliphate and the rise of national sovereignties is a fact and political Islam has found a place for itself within this framework. From the point of view of the Islamic modernist, the process of *ijma* must be a democratic process and as Iqbal says, in order to avoid possibilities of erroneous interpretation of Islam, the reform should take place where it is most needed–the present system of legal education.

Iqbal's *Reconstruction* is a landmark in the history of South Asian Islamic modernism. Fazlur Rahman, unlike Iqbal, holds a unique position in the context of Pakistan. A graduate from the University of Punjab, with doctorate from Oxford, he had received his training both in the East and the West. He was well-versed in the Islamic theological tradition, and a keen student of Islamic and Western literature on the subject. He had an opportunity to have a first hand experience of serving Pakistan as Director of the Islamic Research Institute during the Ayub Khan era. It was an experience which was to be followed by a long expatriate life in the West. His views on various aspects of Islam and Pakistan have already been discussed in this book.

The position of Fazlur Rahman on the question of *riba* is well-known. He had also made a recommendation to revamp the system of *zakat*. He notes that this was the only tax imposed by the Qur'an, and that all the social needs of the Prophet's society were thought to be covered by it. In the framework of a pre-development economy, it was conceived as a wealth tax leviable on the surplus and hoarded wealth of a person. Generally, today it is misunderstood to be a 'poor tax' and it gradually became a voluntary charity when its place was taken by the secular taxation of the modern state (1970: 328ff). He recommended in 1966 that *zakat* should be rationalized, with its rate refixed in view of the colossal increase in government expenditure, and that its application be extended to the sector of investment wealth from merely hoarded wealth, 'thus restoring to the tax-payer his proper Islamic motivation and minimizing tax-evasion...' (p. 328). The proposal aroused a controversy on a national scale, not about its merits but from the ulama for someone daring to tinker with the classical institution. Also, the modernist observers were lukewarm as it seemed to be too abrupt a change in the established practice. Rahman, however, had envisaged a gradual revision in the taxation system of the country.

Fazlur Rahman was an eloquent spokesman for an enlightened change in Islamic thought. He claimed that in order to convey the true message of Islam in modern times, it was necessary to recognize the difference between general principles and specific responses to a'concrete and particular historical situation'. He was of the view that the dogmatists by admitting no change in the Islamic law had created a dangerous situation in the Muslim society. He accused the ruling modernists of acting as a drag on Islamic reform. He questioned the modernist intellectuals about their methods for reinterpreting Islam, suggesting that they were guilty of duplicity, double-talk and 'piece-meal thinking'. He thought that the pressures of moribund conservatives and the imbecilities of Islamic modernists would generate secularism, as the rising middle class might abandon Islam of the conservatives. 'Muslim secularism could, therefore, be possibly conceived as an alternative form, or a phase, of Islamic modernism' (p. 333).

In light of this discussion, I now propose to examine the issue of secularism in the next section.

Scope for Secularism

Secularism and secularization are terms which are used in a variety of meanings. The common perception among the ulama, shared by many Pakistanis, is that secularism is associated with lack of moral values and with lascivious attitudes in the Western societies. This view emanates partly from the superficial knowledge of the Western tradition of religion and politics, and partly from an uncalled-for hubris which ignores the social realities around them. The fact is that the relation between religious belief and ethical behaviour is a very complex phenomenon.

Secularism, in general, refers to that change which occurred in Europe during seventeenth to nineteenth centuries when focus was put on reason, art, aesthetics and poetry, dispensing with the necessity of religion and belief in God. It was a period of widespread profanation. It has a specific connotation as it was employed in the struggle to disengage state from the Church.

In the recent literature, secularization has been used by sociologists to denote the distinction between tradition and modernity, between religious fetishism and superiority of science. It is an illusive concept, however. Glasner (1977) has identified many different and sometimes contradictory meanings which have been assigned to the concept. It is the ideal typical approach which seems to underline a dichotomy which may be over-emphasized, because the social and political factors do not necessarily move in a linear direction. It is important to note that in Western democracies, secularism has not necessarily resulted in shrinkage of religion. Daniel Bell raises an important historical question concerning secularism in England (1980: 331 and fn. 7). With early development of science, with pioneering experience of industrialization, with development of economics 'almost as an English science', there was little of the harsh anti-religious sentiment that arose in France and Germany in the nineteenth century. 'Given the structure of secularization, the wonder of it is why England should have been not the first, but seemingly among the last—in the last decades if we are to believe the 'evidence'—to be secularized' (ibid). Bell did not discuss this historical question—'for that would take us too far afield...'. In the context of my present discussion, however, it might be possible to raise a point to ask how resilient was the religious dogma and the institution of the state in England as compared to Continental Europe and what part this fact played in forming English attitude to the phenomenon. One cannot do justice to this question within the space available here, but it is important to note that with the passage of time, the Western world discovered the sociopolitical functions of secularism, a balance between the forces of state and that of religion. This is quite consistent with the cycles of extraordinary rise in religious enthusiasm in the United States, as it is with Christmas decorations and use of religious rituals at state ceremonies throughout Europe and North America. This is not to deny that at the level of social structure and culture, as Bell suggests, the world has been secularized (p.347). He envisages, however, the rise of new religion or religions, not as regulative forces in their role, but as a basis of existential phenomenon, 'the awareness of men of their finiteness and the inexorable limits to their powers, and the consequent effort to find a coherent answer to reconcile them to that of human condition' (p. 351). Whatever the prospects of Bell's prophecy, his statement underlines another fact, not fully appreciated in the Muslim world, that of philosophic limitations of secularism in the Western societies.

Returning to the role of Islam in Pakistan, the main question is what prospects are there for Islamic modernism in the framework of Iqbal's *Reconstruction* or Fazlur Rahman's sociological approach which raises serious problems of a theological nature about the eternity of the Word of God and Divine Law. '[T]here is no reason to believe that Muslims are ready to accept it', to quote Fazlur Rahman about his own view of Islamic modernism (p. 331).

Secularist tendencies are emerging in the urban areas of Pakistan. It is very difficult to say if these tendencies will gather enough momentum to lead to a possible desacrelization of politics in the country. There is really no example available in this regard in the Muslim world. The secularized Turkey has not inspired other Muslim countries to follow its path to modernity. Ataturk abolished the sultanate which had been elevated to caliphate in Muslim collective consciousness, says Arkoun (1994: 24ff). He attacked the Muslim cultural heritage by dropping Arabic alphabet in favour of Latin, the turban and fez for hat, and the Islamic law for the Swiss legal code. 'Official ceremonies, cooking, furniture, urbanism, the calendar, all those semiological systems that affect individual and collective sensibilities and control the *a priori* forms of understanding, were officially abolished and slated for replacement by European systems in the space of a few years' (p. 25). Ataturk believed that it was enough to take the 'prescriptions' for the success of Western civilization and apply them to Turkey. The country continues to be confronted with the weight of Islam, which interferes more heavily than ever with its availability for Europeanization (p. 26).

There is no secularist tradition in the Islamic political thought. It is surprising because most of the Muslim rulers from the seventh century onward had gained power through wars, intrigues and succession including Mughal Emperor Aurangzeb who is a favourite of the Islamic ideologues. From the point of view of the ulama, the *modus vivendi* with the 'pious' Muslim rulers was based on an understanding which permitted a role for them concerning the basic pillars of Islam such as prayers, fasting, marriage and death in daily life of the Muslims. There is, however, a secularist element in Ibn Khaldun's philosophy of history with regard to *asabiya*. It may be strengthened through a common bond of religion but is not rooted in the belief system. In our own times, Abd ar-Raziq (d.1966) was more explicit about the relation between state and religion. According to his view, the political authority does not belong to the essence of Islam, and that Muslims should be free to choose whatever form of government they would find suitable to enhance their welfare. His opinion created an extremely hostile reaction among the ulama and as punishment he was deprived of his Al-Azhar degree and his judicial appointment (Enayet 1982: 63ff). His main argument is relevant in modern times, however, which describes Prophet's messengership as a spiritual rather than political leadership. It is inherent in the simplicity for conducting the affairs of the Islamic state and in his refusal to leave behind any set of detailed administrative directives for the future Muslim generations. This assertion, as

Rosenthal notes, cuts at the very basis of the claim according to which Islam is an all-inclusive system (Rosenthal 1965: 85ff). There is, however, no agreement on what constitutes an all-inclusive system. The place of the sharia in countries which claim to be Islamic states differs according to differences in doctrinal, ideological and social factors. That is what, for example, differentiates Saudi Arabia from Pakistan, in spite of the attempts made from time to time to emulate some Saudi customs. An important implication of Abd ar-Raziq's view is to shift the responsibility for upholding moral values from the state to the individual. 'The crux of any exaltation of the Prophet's spiritual as opposed to his political or military leadership is that it is also an exaltation of individual conscience versus forcible collective conformism'(Enayet: 68).

There is a wide gap in perceptions about Islam between common people and the elite groups which promote Islamicization in Pakistan. The villager practices Islam in the ordinary business of his life as best as he can. If he is not able to say his prayers as often as he would like to, or to observe fasting during Ramazan, that does not diminish his Muslim-ness (Kurin 1986). Casual observations would indicate that ordinary people in cities follow the same pattern in their religious practices. A Muslim's life at the grassroots level becomes complicated by the fact that the language in which he recites his prayers and reads the Qur'an is mostly incomprehensible to him. In order to cope with his hopes and fears, and his superstitions, he leans on saints and *pirs*. There are economic, social and anthropological factors which explain how the simple belief system—God and the Prophet—gets various interceding elements in it. It is from among the ordinary Muslims, however, that the *madaris* (religious schools, singular: *madrasa*) attract young recruits. These *madaris* started to receive direct funding from the regime of Ziaul Haq which continues to this day. In these institutions, the students learn the basics of fundamentalism and they also get some training in the cause of jihad.

The chattering classes, unlike the common people, seem to be moving away from Islam, as referred to above. They are Westernized in outlook and they send their children for Western-style education. The gap between the two classes is widening.

Islamicization is based on a narrow and literal view of Islam, that of the traditional ulama. During the period of high level of Islamicization in the regime of Ziaul Haq, Pakistan had become a coercive state. The traditional religio-political system is defined as one which meets the following five criteria: ideology is derived entirely from religion; political and religious communities are inseparable and religious conversion is akin to treason; political stability comes from religious legitimacy rather than political capability; religious specialists fill many important political roles; and the political ruler has extensive religious functions (D.E. Smith 1970: 6–7). With the exception of the last factor, the regime of Ziaul Haq largely fulfils the other criteria. And his legacy is very much alive as many of the orders and ordinances introduced by him still carry force of the law. When it is suggested that Islam is not congruent with the modern liberal state (Carroll 1984), it is certainly applicable to that regime.

The Islamic modernists are much less inclined to use authoritarian path towards achieving their goal. They would like to use *ijtehad* for a sustained reinterpretation of jurisprudence, and to arrive at a new understanding of Islam through open debate. They would also like to focus on normative Islam, but to distinguish it from historical Islam in order to emphasize the general moral teachings of the religion. In the opposite camp, there is no tradition of religious-legal intellectual pursuits in Pakistan. There is propagandist religious leadership which was introduced by Maudoodi, and which encourages religio-political disciples hip rather than pursuit of independent religious-legal scholarship. And there are the pulpeteering mullas shrieking about the 'Westernized' classes through megaphones from their mosques. Also, the regional tensions surrounding Pakistan—the Afghan question and the Kashmir issue—continue to encourage and inspire fundamentalist tendencies in the country. Behind the cacophony of traditional Islam, the message is clear: there is no going back on the Objectives Resolution, on the Sharia Act, by means of a deliberate political action. Only through breach rather than observance of the tenets of these guidelines, the secularist tendencies will continue creeping into the culture and the body-politic of the nation.

The political economy of Pakistan will remain in a condition of flux, under these circumstances. Unless the state becomes too coercive in economic matters, the daily business of commerce, industry and finance will continue to proceed through evasive channels, appearing to conform to the Islamic economic rules but going against their purpose. Sound economic policies can evolve only when the principles are clearly defined and universally respected. When the interest paid or charged is called interest, not profit-sharing, a direct and honest framework can be established in which to follow the goals of a sound economic policy. The immediate prospects for Pakistan seem to be to continue preaching the concept of the Islamic state but to observe it more in breach than observance, both in the political and economic spheres of the national life.

Conclusion

Islamic resurgence is a post-World War II phenomenon, and it is associated with search for identity of the newly independent Muslim countries. In its militant form, it is generally ascribed to specific causes such as poverty, social instability and political repression. During the Pakistan movement, to recapitulate the arguments presented in this book, Islam was invoked but its role in the new country was never clearly defined. After 1947, Islam became a useful slogan for the political leaders in order to stem the threat of linguistic and ethnic conflicts in the formative phase of the establishment of Pakistan. This provided a suitable opportunity to the religious ideologues to pursue their goal of the Islamic state as envisaged by them. It would not be an exaggeration to suggest that Abul A'la Maudoodi was an important driving force behind the campaign to convert politics into a branch of theology. The role played by him in order to achieve his objective is well known in the relevant literature (e.g. Binder 1961).

Words and Deeds - I

The dichotomy between the ideal and the vision cherished by a country, whether it is advanced or developing, and the limitations of reality facing the country are obvious facts of history. The Islamic factor adds another complication for Pakistan, somewhat differently from other Muslim countries. First, whether it was to be a Muslim country or an Islamic state is a controversial issue. The Objectives Resolution with its vague and rhetorical pronouncements did not resolve the matter, and in fact contributed to the confusion about it.

Secondly, the birth of Pakistan was a serious challenge; many formidable obstacles in the formation of the new state machinery had to be overcome. Added to this challenge was the refugee problem created by an unprecedented migration of people on both sides of the new frontier dividing the old Punjab into East (Indian) and West (Pakistan) Punjab. This problem was also faced by other provinces, but Punjab received by far the heaviest concentration of new citizens. In order to facilitate their settlement, a system for the assignment of 'evacuee property' was established—the property left behind by Hindus and Sikhs who in general constituted prosperous urban communities in what was to become West Punjab. The evacuee property was allocated on the basis of claims filed by the Muslim migrants. It was suggested at the time, and it is now generally recognized, that a large number of fictitious and exaggerated claims were used to take possession of vacated homes and commercial buildings. Behind the newly instituted system for the settlement of the people, there emerged the use of power for profits, preferment and prestige for the benefit of a few at the expense of the larger interests of the society. This phenomenon established a new pattern of property rights in the country, partly based on the genuine allocation process and partly because of what, according to one definition, may be called corruption (Gould and Kolb 1964). It certainly was not a very auspicious beginning for a homeland, owing to this fetid element, for which the people had flocked around the independence movement and had made immense sacrifices for a dream. It is interesting to note that no studies have been done on this aspect of Pakistan's history, neither concerning the migration nor about the system which was used for the settlement of the new comers.

Words and Deeds - II

It is not my purpose to examine the issue of corruption in detail in this chapter which, according to the high-ranking national politicians, has become a serious problem in the country, especially at the higher echelons of the government.[1] My concern is with the broader issue. Myrdal, for example, has discussed the causes and effects of corruption with reference to South Asia (1968, vol. II, p. 937ff.), and his observations are still relevant today. There is, however, a special problem which has emerged in Pakistan, and that is the preferment, evasion and camouflage which have developed as a response to Islamic reforms. Let me explain with the help of two examples.

The ban on consumption on alcoholic beverages introduced by Z.A. Bhutto during his regime, has resulted in two kinds of responses: smuggling of the contraband goods and the use of permits, which are issued only to non-Muslim citizens. There is a general assumption in the country, that both these sources of supply in fact cater to the demands of the Muslim buyers, making the various brands of the banned product, domestic as well as foreign, available on the basis of their 'scarcity' prices. It is an exchange phenomenon which has established a new class of rent-seekers who nevertheless fulfill an important function in the market. The prohibition has popular support among the ulama who often organize raiding parties on clubs and hotels, especially at festive times to condemn this 'decadence' of the Western society. There is no similar religious zeal about the distribution and use of drugs which seems to have engulfed the country. The ban on liquor, however, has created a stalemate in which hypocrisy seems to provide a link for coexistence among politicians, bureaucrats, the domestic producers (who continue to manufacture alcoholic liquor for beverage), the suppliers, and the affluent consumers of the forbidden product. The situation cannot be examined objectively unless and until the meaning and purpose of the relevant Qur'anic verses is established.

The system of compulsory collection of *zakat* established by General Ziaul Haq had its first challenge when the members of the Shiite community objected to the scheme on the basis of the dictates of their own jurisprudence. An exemption had to be made to accommodate them, and that also opened the door for those non-Shiite Muslims who wanted to take advantage of this loophole by means of a ritual of simple declaration concerning their denominational identity. Others who wish to avoid paying *zakat* are reported to fiddle their bank accounts around the annual due date starting with the month of Ramazan, or use alternative means to hide their assets.

The collection of *zakat* has resulted in serious misallocation of funds, according to media reports. The Ziaul Haq government gave financial assistance to *madaris* (recently made well-known by the Afghan Taliban alumni), which does not fall under the category of charitable donations. From a mere 868 in 1975, these *madaris* grew to 8000 in 1977, the year in which martial law was declared. Recent reports about the allocation of funds for political purpose under the Benazir Bhutto government indicate that the practice has continued, only the objectives may have changed.[2]

Forward to the Past?

The 1973 Constitution required that the financial structure of the country be transformed in accordance with the dictates of Islam. General Ziaul Haq and his supporters, especially those who were appointed to the Council of Islamic Ideology and the Federal Shariat Courts, were taking necessary steps towards rapid Islamicization of the economy. From the time of the Objectives Resolution to the martial law declared by Ziaul Haq there had not been any serious attempt made to discuss or debate the specifics of the Islamic injunctions in a climate of independent thinking. A small opportunity arose during the period of Ayub Khan concerning the question of *riba* but, as discussed in Chapter 2 above, the opposition from Islamic groups brought it to a premature end.

The legacy of Islamic reforms of Ziaul Haq is that banks and related financial institutions are run on the so-called Islamic lines but the vast financial machinery of the government continues to function on the basis of the Western framework. The banks, however, have discovered that they can carry on with their usual business—lending at a higher rate than that paid to the depositors—under a new name. The *raison d'etre* of interest-free financing is that profits should be shared in relation to the direct risk taken by the lender. This rule has disappeared and is buried under the concept of average profits.

The use of various subterfuges (*hiyal*) in order to cope with the criterion of interest-free banking has received strong support from a religious scholar who regards these subterfuges as legitimate activities. Tahirul Qadri, of the Barelvi school offers a broad interpretation of the question in his polemical monograph for the transitional period before the establishment of an Islamic state (1987). He defines *riba* as an excess charged on the postponement or an extension of a loan. In *bay'*, however, there is a clear presumption of sharing the rewards from an investment activity by the owner of the capital with the entrepreneur (pp. 21–5).

He then emphasizes the concept of the asset (*mal*) which is anything used in production and legitimate exchange. In its widest sense, therefore, it includes all notes issued by banks and all certificates created by the government. These items, Qaderi claims, can be used in exchange transactions at prices determined by the market, similar to other assets, and are legitimate activities (pp. 33–42). It is also permissible to sell an asset at a higher price when credit is involved, because credit transaction like cash falls in the category of bay' (p. 64). The bank deposits and loans can also be legitimized through 'partnership' agreements. And if a loss should occur from an enterprise, it could be carried into the next period when profits received would offset it. He supports other instruments of financing such as mark-up, mark-down, and buy-back arrangements. He suggests that there would be no rationale for using *hiyal* if and when a system can be found which would make it possible for entrepreuners to meet the needs of the people without engaging in profit-making activities. Thus, for Qaderi gone is the tying of risk to the actual profits and losses incurred in a given enterprise, to distinguish it from interest-based financing, which is the criterion that started the whole debate on the question of *riba*.

The consequence of Islamicization of banks is that under the thick layer of subterfuges, no meaningful examination can be conducted about the ends and means of monetary policy and its relations with the fiscal framework of the government in the country.

The Hudood Ordinances were introduced in order to establish an Islamic order based on the criteria of Islamic justice. This was in fact an attempt to transplant the classical juristic rules, replacing the existing system as it had evolved during the British rule. There is a consensus in the country that women have become a special target of these Ordinances with reference to the law of evidence and the punishment for *zina*. A contrary opinion was expressed a few years ago (Kennedy 1988) which has now been reprinted in a monograph, published by the pro-Islamicization Institute of Islamic Studies (Kennedy 1996, chapters 2 and 3). Based on convictions made under section 10(2) concerning adultery for the period 1980-84 (p. 63), it is contended that to the extent gender bias is present in the implementation of this provision, it favours women . It is because only 44 per cent of women at the level of the District courts and 30 per cent at the level of the Appellate

Federal Shariat Court were convicted under this crime (p. 73). On surface, the argument seems persuasive, but it is not convincing enough to dispel criticism of the Ordinances. It is disingenuous to suggest that if the intent of this section was to discriminate against women, there would be more of them convicted under this provision than men. Of the one hundred cases mentioned in the above list, conviction of thirty women is not an insignificant figure, in the context of the social milieu of Pakistan. In the patrimonial framework of the society, a man in a dominant position may be able to abuse the honour of a woman with impunity and she may be liable to *hadd* punishment if she happens to become pregnant; the encounter sometimes may be based on acquiescence, but more often than not it would be under duress. In so far as the accusation of adultery can be used to restrict the right of a woman to marry according to her own choice, it sets a standard of morality and a legal precedent for them. The use of statistical averages under these situations would conceal rather than underline the facts. Also, behind the Ordinances is lurking a specific concept of Islamic punishments concerning unlawful intercourse and a false accusation about it (verse 24:2), with punishment of hundred stripes for the former and eighty stripes for the latter crime.

There are two issues involved in this Qur'anic verse. First, of course, is the social context in which the verse was revealed and, secondly, is the question of its relevance in modern times. The underlying message of the Qur'an is categorical, that chastity is a virtue. It is possible to argue that this virtue can be promoted and protected quite effectively by the use of modern institutions such as imprisonment, fines and penalties. With the exception of Wahabi fervour with which countries like Saudi Arabia confront this issue, a majority of Muslim countries have adopted modern means for coping with this situation.

The other issue relates to rules and regulations about marriage and divorce. The Qur'an enunciates basic principles in this matter, leaving considerable scope for the society to establish a proper legal framework for this institution. Also, given the significance of the Qur'anic message in verse 24:2, it is of paramount importance that these rules carry an extensive consensus so that the boundaries of being unmarried, married and divorced are clearly identified. Concerning the first objective, the regime of General Ziaul Haq was indifferent towards the Family Laws Ordinance, unlike other aspects of Islamicization implemented by him. The second objective, it seems, remains unfulfilled.

A recent decision by a judge of the Lahore High Court underlines the dilemma faced by women in this regard.[3] A marriage consummated without the consent of the *wali* (the guardian) is illegal according to this judgment. As the two women who were the subject of this judgement were married without getting this condition fulfilled, they were therefore guilty of *zina* and liable to the corresponding punishment. One of these women was under-age, but the judgement claims to have a general application, whether a woman is unmarried, widowed or divorced. The other judges seem to disagree with their colleague on this matter.

The judgement, nevertheless, underlines the problems of Islamicization. It is asserted by those who want to return to the classical Islamic institutions that these institutions carry a divine authority with them. In fact, they are the product of human endeavour to interpret the moral values in the context of the existing circumstances. What makes the situation even more complex is the fact that behind the consensus of Islamic jurisprudence, there are significant differences of opinion. Pakistan is generally considered to be a Hanafi-based society. The judge who argued for the role of the *wali* in marriage, skirted around the opinion of Imam Abu Hanifa, using opinions of other jurists in support of his position. He also made references to the social pressures on the family system, especially the onslaught of what he called the propaganda of modern media, weakening the Islamic concept of life.

How best then to invoke religion in aid of resolving the social malaise facing the country is the main question. Is it by imposing stricter regulations on women in order to preserve the patriarchal social structure, in the name of the Divine Will, or by educating parents as well as their children about their responsibilities in modern times, in the framework of Islamic values?

The crux of the Islamic order is that there is tension between two concepts which are the pillars of this order: the concept of the Islamic state as a custodian of Islam, on the one hand, with powers encompassing the entire conduct of life and, on the other, the concept of the *homo-Islamicus*—the one who is pious and is driven to good deeds by virtue of his faith in God and the Prophet. There is a contradiction here, as I have already mentioned in this book, because the *homo-Islamicus,* by definition, should need no state regulation for his actions. The message of the Qur'an for commanding good and forbidding evil implies a political order based on egalitarian and just moral principles. What is the relation between the state and the individual, and what is the scope of state action concerning the religious and moral duties of an individual has never been properly addressed in the relevant literature. Historically, the personal responsibilities of the individual have been defined through two broad approaches, the Mu'tazalite and the Ash'arite. According to the former, human being as free agents can distinguish between good and evil by rational means and as such are responsible before a just God. This thesis is best explained by the exegesis of Mahmud b. Umar al-Zamakhshari (d. 1144), whose commentaries have exercised a great influence on the Sunni world of which Pakistan is a part, but whose theological inferences have been opposed or ignored..

The latter school rejects the idea of natural reasoning because good and evil are as God decrees them. The leading exponent of this approach was Fakhrud-Din Razi (d. 1209). An important political implication of Asha'rite view is that God's will should be maintained by compulsion and regulation. As for the Qur'anic verse saying that there is no compulsion in religion (2:256), a majority of the Qur'anic commentators interpret it to mean that only the People of the Book (Jews and Christians) should be left to their religion as long as they pay the *jizya* (poll tax). This interpretation strengthens the Asha'rite position. It may be said that Maudoodi and other Islamic activists in Pakistan are the latter-day Ash'arites.[4]

The idea of congregation, especially for Friday prayers, for the Eid, and the pilgrimage to Mecca for those who can afford it, as well as fasting and *zakat*, provide a basis to promote common concerns of the community of Muslims. The principle of Islamic state, however, based on modern nationalism negates the pan-Islamic sense of the community. The nation-state gives rise to its own forces to maintain itself which are usually largely secular in nature. In fact, a major part of the history of Islam is characterized by a coexistence between the 'pious sultan' and the ulama, each side looking after its domain. Also, not all Muslims in modern times live under the umbrella of an Islamic state. The reality of the partition of British India in 1947 underlines the fact that there are as many Muslims living in the Hindu-dominated India as in Pakistan. On a larger scale, the distinction between *dar-ul-harab* and *dar-ul-Islam* which was used by Islamic jurists in order to advise Muslims not to make their home in the former territories has become meaningless. A large number of Muslims have been migrating voluntarily to western countries in search of better opportunities. It is reasonable to assume that these Muslim migrants do not expect to be treated as zimmies ('protected' citizens).

On the eve of independence, M.A. Jinnah envisaged Pakistan to be a multi-ethnic and multi-religious society. His Speech to the Pakistan Constituent Assembly on August 11, 1947 (see Chapter 2 above) is often quoted as an evidence in this regard. As I have already suggested that he could not have anticipated at that time the scale of refugee problem which would alter the demographic map of the country. Was he then enunciating his views about the role of minorities in the new country now that the battle had been won, or could there be anything deeper about his convictions? Or, was it just the 'cyclone of events' which had disoriented him, as suggested by his recent biographer? It is possible to argue, however, that this would be a superficial assessment about the real man. As a young adult, Jinnah left the Aga Khan's 'Sevener' Khoja community and adopted a Twelver variety of Shia'ism which must have given him a sense of the notion of natural law. He led the rest of his life as a modern non-practising Muslim—qua Muslim, nevertheless. And being so deeply committed to a cause, he must have developed his own views about his Muslim-ness, his sense about the spirit of Islam. Of course, this is all speculation. He was devoted to his politics and whether his religious feelings, however feeble or faint they might have been, played any role in his politics is not an easy question to answer. His own place as a minority (Shia identity) within a minority (Sunni Muslims) could not have escaped him.[5]

The romanticism of the idea of all-encompassing Islamic state, nevertheless, continues to persist, especially getting a new lease under Islamic resurgence. It has not come to grips with the above tension and it is this phenomenon which is undermining the basic framework of civil society in Pakistan.

The question of *zakat* may be used to illustrate the point. Professor Fazlur Rahman has argued in favour of using the principle of *zakat* as a pivot for restructuring government revenue, replacing the existing system of taxation. This proposition would require a careful study before it could be considered as a feasible alternative to the current practice. There is, however, a tradition gradually developed among South Asian Muslims over the last century in which voluntary payment of *zakat* was considered as an important religious duty of individual Muslims. It is not possible to make even a rough estimate of the volume of contributions made in this regard. This sentiment concerning *zakat*, however, could have been given a proper incentive through suitable fiscal measures by the government so that the scope and objectives of charitable donations, both from the point of view of the donor and the recipient, could be clearly defined, perhaps not necessarily as a final solution but as an important incremental measure, thus establishing a point of convergence between the role of the state and the responsibility of the individual. This approach would require, however, that a sympathetic re-examination of the classical Islamic jurisprudence about this, and indeed other issues, is accepted as a paramount necessity. Pakistan is based on the historical progress of the idea in which intellectual contributions of Sir Syed Ahmad Khan and Mohammad Iqbal have played a very important role. They were not pusillanimous men about their convictions. The essential message of both these thinkers is that reconstruction of religious thought in Islam is a *sine qua non* for the survival of Muslim in modern times.

To conclude, Islamicization is based on the assumption that the state must legislate and regulate all aspects of human activity. The Islamic reforms so far introduced do not seem to show any trend towards greater piety among the people, nor have these reforms strengthened unity among the various sects, or the linguistic and ethnic groups. There is such a lack of purpose and a widespread social malaise that Pakistan seems to be a country which is still in search of a nation.

NOTES

1. After the dismissal of Benazir Bhutto's government by the president of Pakistan, the newspaper in the country carried on extensive discussion on the question of corruption and accountability. See, especially *Dawn* and *The News*, various issues of November 1996.
2. There has been coverage of this issue in *Dawn* from time to time, especially in articles by Ardeshir Cowasji. See, for example, *Dawn*, October 31, 1996 about religious schools, and Cowasji about corruption discussed under the title of 'Ehtesab or Intekhab', various issues of December, 1996.
3. The text of the judgement was published in *Dawn*, September 26, 1996. For comments on this judgement see *The Friday Times*, October 3, 1996: Prof. Rafi Ullah Shahab, 'Marriage without guardian's consent—the Islamic viewpoint;' October 10, 1996: Khaled Ahmed, 'The selective wisdom of Justice Cheema;' December 5, 1996: Durdana Soomro, 'Let them marry their husbands.'
4. For discussion about rational thinking on good and evil see George F. Hourani, *Islamic Rationalism: The Ethics of Abd al-Jabbar*, Oxford, Clarendon, 1971, and Abdulaziz A. Sachedina, 'Freedom of Conscience and Religion in the Qur'an', being Chapter 3 in David Little et al., *Human Rights and the Conflict of Cultures: Western* and *Islamic Perspectives on Religious Liberty*, Columbia, S.C., University of South Carolina Press, 1988.
5. See Stanley Wolpert, *Jinnah of Pakistan*, New York, Oxford University Press, 1984 about his comments on Jinnah's speech, p. 340; for a discussion about Jinnah's religious identity, see John Kelsay, 'Saudi Arabia, Pakistan and Universal Declaration of Human Rights,' being Chapter 2 in Little et al., op. cit., especially p. 43ff. and footnote 22.

Glossary

Adl	Justice; in Islamic jurisprudence *al-adl* is used for divine justice.
Ah'san	Benevolence; underlines the spirit of accommodation.
Asabiya	Social solidarity; it is one of the key concepts of Ibn Khaldun's science of culture, underlining common familial bonds.
Bay'	Trade or commercial activity.
Bay' salam	A sale with advance payment for future delivery. In practice a *hila* aimed at legitimizing credit instrument.
Bay' muajjal	Contract for deferred payment. A form of credit instrument. In Pakistan it is also referred to as *morabaha* which in its narrow definition is a sale at a specified profit margin but is now used to describe transaction at an agreed marked-up price.
Dar-ul-Islam	The Abode of Islam; a legal concept denoting land under Islamic law as compared to *dar-ul-harab*: the Abode of War.
Diyat	Blood money for murder or manslaughter. Another *hadd* punishment is *qisas*, 'eye for an eye'.
Fiqah	'Understanding, knowledge', science of Islamic law; jurisprudence.
Gharar	Uncertainty, risk; technically any speculative activity.
Hadd	Islamic punishment; plural *hudood*.
Hila	Technically, lawful means used to reach an unlawful objective. Plural: *hiyal*. In

	jurisprudence it is legal device to accommodate a practice.
Homo Islamicus	One who is driven to good deeds by virtue of his faith in God.
Ijarah	Lease contract; also includes hire purchase system. There are controversies among the jurists about the element of *riba* in a lease or a hire-purchase contract.
Ijma	Consensus within the community, especially among the ulama of a school of law on the interpretation of the *sharia*.
Istihsan	Equity, a concept emphasising egalitarian value.
Khiyar al-ru'ya	The option for transaction after inspection.
Madrasa	School for educating Muslims in religious science such law, Qur'an, traditions.
Majlis-e-shoora	Consultative assembly, underlines the authority of the head of the state.
Muzara'a	Sharecropping tenancy; the other arrangement is mazarabat in which excess land is given in rent on profit-sharing basis.
Mehr	Dowry, bridal money.
Modaraba	Commanda partnership, trust financing; profits are shared in agreed proportion; loss is borne by the financier according to his share; in modern *modarabas* profits are not tied to specific projects and the risks involved in these projects.
Morabaha	Cost-plus-profit contract.
Mulla	An Urdu derivative of *Mawla*, a learned man; often used for a local religious leader.
Musharaka	Partnership; the profits are shared but are not necessarily identified in relation to each project in a multiproject enterprise.

Purda	A curtain, screen or veil, it is also the virtue of modesty for women.
Qarze-e-hasna	Interest-free loan.
Riba	Unlawful gain by way of excess or deferment. traditionalist ulama include modern interest in this category.
Riba al-fazl	*Riba* by way of increase or excess; it may arise in exchange of commodities and in commercial transactions.
Riba al-nasi'a	*Riba* by way of deferment, also referred to as the Qur'anic *riba*.
Sadaqah	Voluntary alms-giving.
Sarraf	From *sarf* (exchange of currencies); dealer in coins and banking; more extensive activity was performed by the *jahabizah*.
Sharia	The path to be followed; the sacred law of Islam.
Shia	Partisans; those who believe that the Prophet passed on his authority to his cousin and son-in-law, Ali ibn Abi Talib. For *sunnis*, he is one of the pious caliphs.
Sunna	Strictly, traditions of the Prophet. It is also used to distinguish the mainstream Muslim sect—*sunnis*.
Talfiq	A process by which a new law is formed by combining the best parts of some existing laws.
Tawhid	The divine unity. Strictly, monotheism, and for some a holistic world view in *ilm-e-kalam*.
Umma	Community, either in ethno-centric sense, or moe commonly, in religious sense.
Ushr	A tenth or a tithe of the produce for the *baitul mal*.
Wali	A guardian; according to custom and also view of the traditionalist ulama, *wali* plays a role in representing the woman, especially in marriage.

Zakat   Tax levied on the gross assets of Muslims,
                 a religious duty.

Zina   An Islamic legal term for fornication;
                 sexual relations between those not in a
                 state of legal matrimony; historically
                 customary concubinage was excluded
                 from this definition.

Bibliography

Abu-Lughod, Janet L. 1989, *Before European Hegemony: The World System A.D. 1250-1350*, New York, Oxford University Press.

Ahmed, Ishtiaq, 1987, *The Concept of the Islamic State: An Analysis of Ideological Controversy in Pakistan*, London, Prances Printer.

Ahmed, Justice (Retd.) Qadeeruddin, 1994, *What is Riba?* Karachi, Saleemco Printers.

Ahmed, Leila, 1992, *Women and Gender in Islam: Historical Roots of a Modern Debate*, New Haven, Yale University Press.

Ahmed, Talat, 1984, 'Legal Rights of Women in Islam,' Magazine Section, *The Pakistan Times*, November 2.

Ahmed, Zafaryab, 1985, 'Maudoodi's Islamic State,' in Muhammad Asghar Khan, ed., *Islam, Politics and the State: The Pakistan Experience*, London, Zed Books.

Ahmed, Ziauddin, et al., eds., *Money and Banking in Islam*, Islamabad, Institute of Policy Studies.

Alavi, Hamza, 1983, 'Class and State in Pakistan,' in Hassan Gardezi and Jamil Rashid, eds., Pakistan: The Unstable State, Lahore, Vanguard.

Al-Gilani, Manazir Ahsan, 1947, *Islami Ma'ashi'at*, in Urdu; (English translation, Islamic economics), Hyderabad, Duccan, *Idara Isha'at-e-Urdu*.

Al-Qa'deri, Muhammad Tahir, 1987, '*Bila Sood Bank-Kari: Oboori Khakha*, in Urdu; (English translation: 'Interest-free Banking, a Transitional Outline), Lahore, *Ida'ra Minhaj-al-Qur'an*.

Ali, Mahfooz, 1992, 'Islamic Banking: *Riba*, Interest and Profit Sharing,' *Economic Review*, Karachi, September.

Ali, Salamat, 1981a, 'A Matter of Interest', *Far Eastern Economic Review*, January 12.

———, 1981b, 'Crying Out for a Model', *Far Eastern Economic Review*, January 12.

———, 1981c, 'The Semantics of Usury', *Far Eastern Economic Review*, January 12.

Ali, Syed Ameer, 1927, *A Short History of Saracens*, London, Macmillan.

———, 1935, *The Spirit of Islam*, London.

———, 1986, *Muhammadan Law: Complied from Authorities in the Original Arabic*, 4th edn., New Delhi, Himalayan Books.

Amin, Samir, 1993, 'Can Environmental Problems be Subject to Economic Calculations', *Monthly Review*, 45: 7.

Anderson, Benedict, 1983, *Imagined Communities: Refelection on the Origin and Spread of Nationalism*, London, Verso/NLB.

Anderson, Graydon K., 1980, 'On the Poverty of Economics: The Pygmallion Syndrom', *American Economist*, 24: 2.

Anderson, J.N.D., 1959, *Islamic Law in the Modern World*, New York, New York University Press.

———, 1965, 'Recent Reform in the Islamic Law of Inheritance', *International and Comparative Law Quarterly*, 14.

Arkoun, Mohammed, 1994, *Rethinking Islam: Common Questions, Uncommon Answers*, translated and edited by Robert D. Lee, Boulder, Westview Press.

Arrow, Kenneth, 1982, 'Risk Perception in Psychology and Economics, *Economic Inquiry*, January.

Ayubi, Nazih, 1991, *Political Islam: Religion and Politics in the Arab World*, London Routledge.

Aziz, Khurshid Kamal, 1987, *A History of the Idea of Pakistan*, vols. I-III, Lahore, Vanguard.

———, 1993, *The Murder of History in Pakistan*, Lahore, Vanguard.

Bardhan, P.K., 1979, 'Agricultural Development and Land Tenancy in a Peasant Economy: A Theoretical and Empirical Analysis', *American Journal of Agriculrtural Economics*, 61.

―――, 1980, 'Interlocking Factor Markets and Agrarian Development: A Review of Issues', *Oxford Economic Papers*, 38.

―――, and Srinivasan, 1971, 'Cropsharing Tenancy in Agriculture: A Theoretical and Empirical Analysis', *American Economic Review*, March.

Baumol, William J. 1977, *Economic Theory and Operations Analysis*, 4th edn., Englewood Cliff, Prentice-Hall.

Behdad, Sohrab, 1992, 'Property Rights and Islamic Economic Approaches', in Jomo, K.S., ed., *Islamic Economic Alternatives: Critical Perspective and New Directions*, London, Macmillan.

Bell, Daniel, 1980, 'The Return of the Sacred? The Argument on the Future of Religion', *Winding Passage: Essays and Sociological Journneys*, New York, Basic Books.

Belshaw, C.S., 1964, 'Social,Structural and Cultural Values as Related to Economic Growth', *International Social Science Journal*, 16: 2

Binder, Leonard, 1961, *Religion and Politics in Pakistan*, Berkeley, University of California Press.

Birnie, Arthur, 1952, *The History and Ethics of Interest*, London, Hodge.

Bohm-Bawerk, Eugen von, 1922, *Capital and Interest*, translated by William Smart, London, Macmillan.

Bohm-Bawerk, Eugen von, 1923, *Postive Theory of Capital*, translated by William Smart, New York, Stechert.

Boularès, Habib, 1990, *Islam: The Fear and the Hope*, London, Zed Press.

Bromwich, Michael, 1976, *The Economics of Capital Budgeting*, Harmondworth, Penguin.

Buchanan, James and Tullick, Gordon, 1962, *The Calculus of Consent*, Ann Arbor, University of Michigan Press.

Butt, Asghar, 1982, 'Where Should She Be,' *The Pakistan Times*, April 6.

Çagatay, Nes'et, 1970, 'Riba and Interest Concept and Banking in Ottoman Empire, *Studia Islamica*, 32.

Caperoso, James A., and Levine David P., 1992, *Theories of Political Economy*, New York, Cambridge University Press.

Carroll, Lucy, 1982, 'Nizam-i-Islam: Pricesses and Conflicts in Pakistan's Programme of Islamization with Special Reference to the Problems of Women', *Journal of Commonwealth and Comparative Politics*, 20: 1

Carroll, T.G., 1984, 'Secularization and State of Modernity', *World Politics*, 36.

Chapra, M. Umar, 1985, *Towards a Just Monetary System*, Leicester, The Islamic Foundation.

———, 1992, *Islam and the Economic Challenge*, Leicester, The Islamic Foundation.

Chaudhry, Gulnaz, 1987, 'Fair Sex in Unfair Business', Magazine Section, *The Pakistan Times*, August 28.

Cheung, S.N.S., 1968, 'Private Property Rights and Sharecropping', *Journal of Political Economy*, 76, November.

———, 1969, *The Theory of Share Tenancy*, Chicago, University of Chicago Press.

Choudhury, Masudul Alam, 1986, *Contributions to Islamic Economic Theory: A Study in Social Economics*, London, Macmillan.

———, 1992, *The Principles of Islamic Political Economy: A Methodological Inquiry*, New York, St. Martin's Press.

———, and Malik, Uzir Abdul, 1992, *The Foundations of Islamic Economy*, Houndsmills, Macmillan.

Coase, R.H., 1960, 'The Problem of Social Cost', *Journal of Law and Economics*, 3, October.

———, 1974, 'The Lighthouse in Economics', *Journal of Law and Economics*, 3, October.

Cobhem, David, 1992, 'Finance for Development and Islamic Banking', *Intereconomics*, October.

Conard, Joseph W., 1963, *An Introduction to the Theory of Interest*, Bekeley, University of California Press.

Cornelisse, Peter A., and Steffelar, Wouter, 1995, 'Islamic Banking in Practice: the Case of Pakistan', *Development and Change*, 26

Coulson, N.J. 1971, *Succession in the Muslim Family*, Cambridge, Cambridge University Press

Crone, Patricia, 1987, *Meccan Trade and the Rise of Islam*, Princeton, Princeton University Press.

Dalton, George, 1974, *Economic Systems and Society: Capitalism, Communism and the Third World*, Harmondsworth, Penguin.

Desai, Meghnad, 1979, *Marxian Economics*, Totowa, Littlefield, Adams and Co.

Deyo, F.C. ed., 1987, *The Political Economy of the New Asian Industrialization*, Ithaca, Cornell, University Press.

Dwyer, Larry, 1982, 'Value Freedom and the Scope of Economic Inquiry', *American Journal of Economics and Sociology*, 41:2.

_____, 1982, 'The Alleged Value Neutrality of Economics: An Alternative View', *Journal of Economic Issues*, 16:1

Elster, J., 1985, *Making Sense of Marx*, Cambridge, Cambridge University Press.

Enayat, Hamid, 1982, *Modern Islamic Political Thought*, Austin, University of Texas Press.

Feldman, Herbert, 1967, *Revolution in Pakistan: A Study of the Martial Law Administration*, London, Oxford University Press.

Fyzee, A.A.A., 1974, *Outlines of the Muhammadan Law*, Delhi, Oxford University Press.

Galbraith, J. Kenneth, 1958, *The Affluent Society*, 4th edn., 1984, New York, Houghton Mifflin.

_____, 1967, *The New Industrial State*, 4th edn., 1985, New York, Houghton Mifflin.

_____, 1992, *The Culture of Contentment*, Boston and New York, Houghton Mifflin.

Gellner, E., 1983, *Nations and Nationalism*, Oxford, Blackwell.

————, ed., 1985, *Islamic Dilemmas: Reformers, Nationalists and Industrialization*, Berlin, Mouton.

Gerth, H.H., and Mills, C. Wright, eds., 1958, *From Max Weber: Essays in Sociology*, New York, Galaxy.

Ghatak, S. 1976, *Rural Money Markets in India*, Delhi, Macmillan.

Gibb, H.A.R., 1947, *Modern Trends in Islam*, Chicago, University of Chicago Press.

Gieraths, Christine, 1990, 'Pakistan: Main Participants and Final Financial Products of the Islamization Process', in Rodney Wilson, ed., 1990, *Islamic Financial Markets*, London, Routledge.

Gintis, H., 1972, 'A Radical Analysis of Welfare Economics and Industrial Development', *Quarterly Journal of Economics*, 86, November.

Glasner, Peter E., 1977, *The Sociology of Secularisation: A Critique of a Concept*, London, Rourledge and Kegan Paul.

Goitein, S.D., 1966, *Studies in Islamic History and Institutions*, Leiden, Brill.

Gotlieb, Manuel, 1984, *A Theory of Economic Systems*, Orlando, Academic Press.

Gould, Julius and Kolb, William L., eds. 1964, *A Dictionary of the Social Sciences*, New York, Free Press.

Habib Bank Ltd., 1986, *Towards Understanding Non-Interest Based Banking in Pakistan*, 2nd edn., Karachi, Habib Bank.

Hagen, E.E., 1962, *On the Theory of Social Change*, Homewood, Dorsey Press.

Hakim, Dr. Khalifa Abdul, 1953, *Islamic Ideology: The Fundamental Beliefs and Principles of Islam and Other Approaches to Practical Life*, Lahore, Institute of Islamic Culture. (This edition has been used for reference in the text. There are some changes in the later editions which are not of relevance to my argument. The 8th edition was published in 1994).

Halliday, Fred, 1979, *Iran: Dictatorship and Development*, Harmondsworth, Penguin.

_____, and Alavi, Hamza, eds., 1988, *State and Ideology in the Middle East*, London, Macmillan Education.

Haque, Ziaul, 1977, *Landlord and Peasant in Early Islam*, Islamabad, Islamic Research Institute.

_____, 1985, *Islam and Feudalism: The Economics of Riba, Interest and Profit*, Lahore, Vanguard. (This edition is used for references in the text. The second edition was published under the title of *Riba: The Moral Economy of Usury, Interest and Profit*, S. Abdul Majeed & Co., for Ikraq, Kuala Lumpur, 1995).

_____, 1992, 'Nature and Methodology of Islamic Economics: An Appraisal,' *The Pakistan Development Review*, 31: 4, Winter.

_____, 1993, 'The Nature and Significance of the Medieval and Modern Interpretation of *Riba*', *The Pakistan Development Review*, 32: 4, Winter.

Hardie, Alexander and Rabooy, M., 1991, 'Risk, Piety, and the Investor', *British Journal of Middle Eastern Studies*, 18: 1.

Hassan, Riffat, 1987, 'Equal Before Allah/Woman-Man Equality in Islamic Tradition', *Harvard Divinity Bulletin*, 17:2, reprinted in *Diva*, 1: 1, April 1988.

Hawkins, C.J., and Pearce, D.W., 1971, *Capital Investment Appraisal*, London, Macmillan.

Hayek, F.F., 1944, *Road to Serfdom*, London, Routledge and Sons.

Hechter, M., 1975, *Internal Colonialism. The Celtic Fringe in British National Development*, London, Routledge.

_____, 1985, 'Internal Colonialism Revisited', in Tirakian, Edward E., and Rogowski, Christian, eds., *New Nationalism of the Developed West*, London, Allen and Unwin.

Heilbroner, Robert, 1992, *Twenty-First Century Capitalism*, Concord (Ont.), Anansi.

Hirsch, Fred., 1978, *Social Limits to Growth*, Cambridge, Mass., Harvard University Press.

Hoodbhoy, Pervez, 1991, *Islamic Science: Religious Orthodoxy and the Battle for Rationality*, London, Zed Books.

Hudson, Michael C., 1980, 'Islam and Political Development', in Esposito, John. L., *Islam and Development: Religion and Sociopolitical Change*, Syracuse, Syracuse University Press.

Human Rights Commission of Pakistan, 1991, *Newsletter*, July.

Hungtington, S.P., 1968, *Political Order in a Changing Society*, New Have, Yale University Press.

Ibrahim, Mahmood, 1980, *Merchant Capital and Islam*, Austin, University of Texas Press.

Imran, Muhammad, 1990, *Ideal Woman in Islam*, 6th edn., Lahore, Islamic Publications.

Iqbal, Sir Muhammad, 1951, *The Reconstruction of Religious Thought in Islam*, Lahore, Shaikh Muhammad Ashraf.

Iqbal, Zubair and Mirakhor, Abbas, 1987, *Islamic Banking*, Occasional Paper 49, Washington DC., International Monetary Fund.

Islam, Zafarul, 1989, 'Banking Activities in the Abbasid Period', *Islam and the Modern Age*, 10: 3, August.

Jafri, Sadiq, 1986, 'Personality Interview', *The Herald*, Karachi, March.

Jahan, Rounaq, 1972, *Pakistan's Failure in National Integration*, New York, Colombia University Press.

Jalal, Ayesha, 1985, *The Sole Spokesman: Jinnah, the Muslim League and the Demand for Pakistan*, Cambridge, Cambridge University Press.

———, 1990, *The State of Martial Law Rule: The Origins of Pakistan's Political Economy of Defence*, Cambridge, Cambridge University Press.

_____, 1995, 'Conjuring Pakistan: History as Official Imagining', *International Journal of Middle East Studies*, 27.

Johnson, C., 1987, 'Political Institutions and Economic Progress: The Government-Business Relations in Japan, South Korea and Taiwan', in Deyo, F.C., ed., *The Political Economy of New Asian Industrialism*, New York, Cornell University Press.

Johnson, D.G., 1950, 'Resource Allocation in Share Contracts', *Journal of Political Economy*, 58, April.

Johnson, Harry G., 1962, *Money, Trade and Economic Growth*, 2nd edn., 1964, London, Allen and Unwin.

Jomo, K.S., 1977, 'Islam and Weber: Rodinson on the Implications of Religion for Capitalist Development', *The Developing Economies*, 15: 4.

Karsten, Ingo, 1982, 'Islam and Financial Intermediation', *Staff Papers*, International Monetary Fund, March.

Katouzian, Homa, 1980, *Ideology and Methods in Economics*, London, Macmillan.

Katouzian, Homayoun, 1981, 'Riba and Interest in an Islamic Political Economy', *Peoples Mediterraneans*, 14, January-March.

Kazarian, Elias G., 1993, *Islamic versus Traditional Banking: Financial Innovation in Egypt*, Boulder, Westview Press.

Kedourie, E. 1960, *Nationalism*, London, Hutchinson.

Kennedy, Charles, 1988, 'Islamization in Pakistan: Implementation of the Hudood Ordinances', *Asian Survey*, March.

_____, 1990, 'Islamization and Legal Reform in Pakistan, 1979-1989', *Pacific Affairs*, 63: 1.

_____, 1993, 'Islamization of Real Estate: Pre-Emption and Land Reform in Pakistan, 1978-1992', *Journal of Islamic Studies*, January.

_____, 1996, *Islamization of Laws and Economy: Case Studies on Pakistan*, Islamabad, Institute of Policy Studies.

Key Law Reports, 1992, 'Federal Shariat Court Judgement, 9th July and 24th October, 1991, Mahmood-ur-Rahman Faisal versus Secretary, Ministry of Law and Justice, and another', [known as Shariat Court ruling concerning elimination of *riba*].

Khadduri, Majid, 1986, *The Islamic Conception of Justice*, Baltimore, Johns Hopkins University Press.

Khan, Ashfaque H., 1988, 'Financial Repression, Financial Development and Structure of Savings in Pakistan', *The Pakistan Development Review*, 27: 4 (Winter)

Khan, Mazhar ul Haq, 1972, *Purdah and Polygamy: A Study in the Social Pathology of the Muslim Society*, Peshawar Cantt., Nashiran-e-Ilm-o-Taraqiyat.

Khan, Mohsin, S., 1986, 'Islamic Interest-Free Banking', *IMF Staff Paper*, March.

Khan, Muhammad Asghar, ed., 1985, *Islam, Politics and the State: The Pakistan Experience*, London, Zed Press.

Khan, Shahrukh Rafi, 1987a, 'An Economic Analysis of PLS Model for the Financial Sector', in Khan Mohsin, S. and Mirakhor, Abbas, eds., *Theoretical Studies in Islamic Banking and Finance*, Houston, Institute for Reseach and Islamic Studies.

———, 1987b, 'The Pakistan Experience with Islamic (Profit-and-Loss Sharing) Banking, *The Bangladesh Development Studies*, 15: 4, December.

Khan, Waqar Masud, 1985, *Towards an Interest-Free Islamic Economic System*, Leicester, The Islamic Foundation.

Killick, T., 1989, *A Reaction Too Far: Economic Theory and the Role of the State in Developing Countries*, London, Overseas Development Institute.

Kuran, Timor, 1983, 'Behavioral Norms in the Islamic Doctrine of Economics', *Journal of Economic Behavior and Organization*, 4.

———, 1986, 'The Economic System in Contemporary Islamic Thought: Interpretation and Assessment', *International Journal of Middle East Studies*, 18.

———, 1989, 'Economic Justice in Contemporary Islamic Thought', *International Journal of Middle East Studies*, May.

———, 1995, 'Islamic Economics and the Islamic Subeconomy', *Journal of Economic Perspectives*, 9: 4 (Fall).

Kurin, Richard, 1985, 'Islamization in Pakistan: A View from the Countryside', *Asian Survey*, August.

———, 1987, 'Islamization: A view from the Countryside', in Weiss, Anita, M., *Islamic Reassertion in Pakistan: The Application of Islamic Laws in a Modern State*, Lahore, Vanguard.

Lahore Law Times, n.d., *The Constitution of Pakistan, 1973: Incorporating All Amendments Update*, Lahore.

———, *The Companies Ordinance, 1984*, Lahore.

Lammens, H. 1924, *La Mecque a la veille l'Hegire*, Beirut.

Lancaster, Kevin, 1966, 'A new Approach to Consumer Theory', *Journal of Political Economy*, 74.

Langé, Oscar, 1945, 'The Scope and Method of Economics', *Review of Economic Studies*, XIII (1945-46).

Leftwich, Adrian, 1994, 'Governance, the State and the Politics of Development', *Development and Change*, 25:2.

Lewis, W. Arthur, 1954, 'Economic Development with Unlimited Supplies of Labour', *Manchester School*, 22, May.

Mahmood, Safdar, 1975, *Constitutional Foundations of Pakistan*, Lahore, Publishers United.

Mahmood, Sh. Shaukat, 1986, *Muslim Family Laws*, 10th edn., Lahore, Legal Research Centre.

Malik, Ghulam Akbar, 1991, *Aurat ka Mukaddama: Islam ki Ada'lat Mein*, in Urdu; in English translation, 'The case of Woman, in the Court of Islam'. Lahore, Jang Publishers.

Malik, Ayesha, 1997, 'Brothers Continue to Gobble Up Sisters' Inheritance', Magazine Section, *Dawn*, December 7.

Mannan, Muhammad Abdul, 1986, *Islamic Economics: Theory and Practice*, rev. edn., Dunton Green, Hodder and Stroughton.

Mansfield, Edwin, 1970, *Microeconomics: Theory and Applications*, New York, Norton, 4th edn., 1982.

Mansoor Books House, n.d., *Important Laws, 1980*, Lahore.

Marshall, Alfred, 1961, *Principles of Economics*, 9th variorum edn., London, Macmillan.

Maryam, Tahira, 1987, 'Beating of Women', Magazine Section, *The Pakistan Times*, October 2.

Maudoodi, Abul A'la, 1967, *Purdah*, in Urdu; (English translation, 'The Veil'), 12th edn.; the 1st edn. was published in 1940. Lahore, Islamic Publications.

_____, 1983, *Ma'ashi'at-e-Islam*, in Urdu; (English translation, 'Islamic Economics'), edited by Khurshid Ahmad, Lahore, Islamic Publications.

_____, 1984, *Sood*, in Urdu; (English translation, 'Interest'), 1961 edition, with several reprints, Lahore, Islamic Publications.

_____, 1994, *Mas'ala Milkiyat-e-Zameen*, in Urdu; (English translation, 'The Question of Land Ownership'), ninth print, edn., Lahore, Islamic Publications.

McKinnon, R.I., 1973, *Money and Capital in Economic Development*, New York, Oxford University Press.

Meenai, S.A., 1984, *Money and Banking in Pakistan*, 3rd edn., Karachi, Allied Book Corporation.

Mehdi, Rubia, 1994, *The Islamization of the Law in Pakistan*, London, Curzon Press

Mermelstein, David, edn., 1973, *Economics: Mainstream Readings and Radical Critiques*, 2nd edn., New York, Random House.

Mernissi, Fatima, 1975, *Beyond the Veil: Male-Female Dynamics in Modern Muslim Society*, Cambridge, Mass., Shankman Publishing Company; rev. edn., 1987, Bloomington, Indiana University Press.

_____, 1991, *The Veil and the Male Elite: A Feminist Interpretation of Women's Rights in Islam*, translated by

Mary Jo Lakeland, Redding, Addison Wesley. Also published under the title of *Women and Islam: An Historical and Theological Enquiry*, Oxford, Basil Blackwell.

Mirza, Anis, 1984, 'Images of Women in the Social and Cultural Life', Magazine Section, *The Pakistan Times*, September 21.

Modigliani, F., and Miller, M.H., 1958, 'The Cost of Capital, Corporation Finance and the Theory of Investment', *American Economic Review*, 48.

Mohammad, Faiz, 1991, 'Prospects of Poverty Eradication Through the Existing *Zakat* System in Pakistan', *The Pakistan Development Review*, 30:4, Part II, Winter.

Morishima, Michio, 1982, *Why Has Japan Succeeded?'*, London, Cambridge University Press.

Mueller, Dennis C., 1979, *Public Choice*, Cambridge, Cambridge University Press.

Mumtaz, Khawar, and Shaheed, Farida, eds., 1987, *Women of Pakistan: Two Steps Forward, One Step Back?*, London, Zed Press.

Munir, Muhammad, 1979, *From Jinnah to Zia*, Lahore, Vanguard Books.

Myrdal, Gunnar, 1968, *Asian Drama: An Inquiry into the Poverty of Nations*, vols. 1-III, New York, Pantheon.

———, 1969, *The Political Elements in the Development of Economic Theory*, New York, Simon and Schuster.

Nabi, Ijaz, 'Contracts, Resource Use and Productivity in Sharecropping', *Journal of Development Studies*, 22:2, January.

Naqvi, Syed Nawab Haider, 1981a, 'Economics of Human Rights: An Islamic Perspective', *Hamdard Islamicus*, Summer.

———, 1981b, *Ethics and Economics: An Islamic Synthesis*, Leicester, The Islamic Foundation.

———, 1994, *Islam, Economics, and Society*, London, Kegan Paul.

_____, et al. *An Agenda on Islamic Economic Reform*, (Report of the Committee on Islamization appointed by the Finance Minister of Pakistan), Islamabad, Institute of Development Economics.

Nasr, Seyyed Vali Reza, 1989, 'Islamic Economics: Novel Perspectives', *Middle Eastern Studies*, 25:4, October.

Nelson, Cynthia, 1974, 'Public and Private Politics: Women in the Middle Eastern World, *American Ethnologist*, 1:1, February.

Newbury, D.M.G., 1975, 'The Choice of Rental Contracts in Peasant Agriculture', in Reynold, L., ed., *Agriculture in Development Theory*, New Haven, Yale University Press.

Nomani, Fahad, and Rehnema, Ali, 1994, *Islamic Economic Systems*, London, Zed Press.

Noonan, Jr., John T., 1957, *The Scholastic Analysis of Usury*, Cambridge, Mass., Harvard University Press.

Pakistan and Gulf Economists, 1993, 'The Modaraba 'industry' in Pakistan', April 24.

Pal, Izzud-Din, 1987, 'Pakistan, Islam and Economics', *Journal of Contemporary Asia*, 17:2.

_____, 1990, 'Women and Islam in Pakistan', *Middle Eastern Studies*, 26:4.

_____, 1994, 'Pakistan and the Question of *Riba*', *Middle Eastern Studies*, 30:1.

Papenek, Hanna, 1973, 'Purdah: Separate Worlds and Symbolic Shelter', *Comparative Studies in Society and History*, June.

Pastner, Stephen, 1987, 'Cultural Barriers to Pakistan's Quest for Unity', *Journal of Developing Societies*, 3.

Patel, Rashida, 1986, *Islamization of Laws in Pakistan*, Karachi, Faiza Publishers.

Pigou, A.C., 1952, *The Economics of Welfare*, 4th edn., London, Macmillan.

Presley, J.R., and Sessions, J.G., 1994, 'Islamic Economics: The Emergence of a New Paradigm', *Economic Journal*, May.

Pryor, Frederick L., 1985, 'The Islamic Economic System', *Journal of Comparative Economics*, 9.

Quibria, M.G., and Rashid, Salim, 1984, 'The Puzzle of Sharecropping: A Survey of Theories', *World Development*, 12:2.

Qureshi, Anwar Iqbal, 1946, *Islam and the Theory of Interest*, Lahore, Shaikh Muhammad Ashraf.

Rahman, Fazlur, 1964, 'Riba and Interest', *Islamic Studies*, 3:4. English translation of 'Tahqiq-i-Riba', in Urdu, *Fikr-o-Nazar*, November 1963.

————, 1966, *Islam*, New York, Holt, Rinehart and Winston.

————, 1967, 'Implementation of the Islamic Concept of State in the Pakistan Milieu', *Islamic Studies*, 6:3.

————, 1970, 'Islamic Modernism: the Scope, Method and Alternatives', *International Journal of Middle East Studies*, 1.

————, 1973, 'Islam and the New Constitution of Pakistan', *Journal of Asian and African Studies*, 8.

————, 1982, *Islam and Modernity: Transformation of an Intellectual Tradition*, Chicago, University of Chicago Press.

————, 1983, 'Status of Women in Islam - II', Magazine Section, *The Pakistan Times*, Lahore, February 4.

Rahman, Muhammad Hifzur, 1951, *Islam ka Iqtisa'di Nizam*, in Urdu; in English translation, 'The Economic System of Islam', 4th printing, Delhi, *Nadwatul Mussanifin*.

Rawls, John, 1971, *A Theory of Justice*, Cambridge, Mass., Harvard University Press.

Rhoads, Steven, 1989, *The Economist's View of the World*, Cambridge, Mass., Harvard University Press.

Robinson, Joan, 1964, *Economic Philosophy*, Harmonsworth, Penguin.

Rosenthal, E.I.J., 1965, *Islam in the Modern National State*, Cambridge, Cambridge University Press.

Rostow, W.W., 1971, *The Stages of Economic Growth*, 2nd edn., Cambridge, Cambridge University Press.

Roy, Ramashray, 1992, 'Modern Economics and the Good Life: A Critique', *Alternatives*, 17:3.

Runge, Calisle Ford, 1986, 'Common Property and Collective Action in Economic Development', *World Development*, 14:5.

Sadowski, Yahya, 1993, 'The New Orientalism and the Democracy Debate', *Middle East Report*, July-August.

Saeed-uz-Zafar, Khwaja, n.d., *Banking Laws Manual*, Lahore, Law Times Publications.

Saleh Nabil A., 1986, *Unlawful Gain and Legitimate Profit in Islamic Law*, Cambridge, Cambridge University Press.

Samuelsson, Kurt, 1957, *Religion and Economic Activity: A Critique of Max Weber*, New York, Harper.

Scandizzo, P.L. 1979, 'Implications for Sharecropping for Technology Design in Northeast Brazil', in Vaddes, A., et al., eds., *Economics and the Design of Small Farmer Technology*, Ames, Iowa State University Press.

Schacht, Joseph, 1953, 'Sharia', *Shorter Encyclopaedia of Islam*, Leiden, Brill.

Schoefller, Sudney, 1952, 'Note on Modern Welfare Economics', *American Economic Review*, 42.

Sen, Amartya, 1987, *On Ethics and Economics*, Oxford, Basil Blackwell.

Shah, Syed Yaqub, 1967, *Chand Ma'ashi Masa'il aur Islam*, in Urdu; (English translation:'Some Economic Issues and Islam', Lahore, *Idara-e-Sadafat-e-Islamia*.

Shah, Nasra M., 1986, 'Change in Female Role in Pakistan: Are the Volume and Pace Adequate', *Pakistan Development Review*, 25:3.

Shah, E.S. 1973, *Financial Deepening in Economic Development*, New York, Oxford University Press.

Shehab, Rafiullah, 1986, *Rights of Women in Islamic Shariah*, Lahore, Indus Publishing House.

Sheikh, Nasir Ahmad, 1961, *Some Aspects of the Constitution and the Economics of Islam*, 3rd edn., Woking, Woking Muslim Mission and Library Trust.

Siddiqi, Muhammad Mazheruddin, 1966, *Women in Islam*, Lahore, Institute of Islamic Culture. (The 11th edition was published in 1996. It is in fact a reprint of the original edition).

Siddiqi, M. Nejatullah, 1970, *Some Aspects of the Islamic Economy*, Lahore, Islamic Publications.

_____, 1981, *Muslim Economic Thinking: A Survey of Contemporary Literature*, Leicester, The Islamic Foundation.

Smith, Adam, 1937, *The Wealth of Nations*, New York, Modern Library.

Smith, Donald E., 1970, *Religion and Political Development*, Boston, Little Brown.

_____, 1971, *Religion, Political and Social Change in the Third World: A Sourcebook*, New York, Free Press.

Solow, Robert M., 1963, *Capital Theory and the Rate of Return*, Amsterdam, North-Holland.

Srinivanan, T.N., 1979, 'Agricultural Backwardness under Semi-Feudalism-Comment', *Economic Journal*, 89.

State Bank of Pakistan, 1980, 'Report on the Elimination of Interest from the Economy, Panel of Economists and Bankers', Karachi.

_____, 1984, 'Permissible Modes of Financing', Annexure-I, *Bulletin*, September.

_____, 1985a, Banking Control Department, Circulars, Karachi.

_____, 1985b, *Bulletin*, December.

_____, 1987, Banking Control Department, Circulars.

Tibi, Bassam, 1985, *Islam and the Cultural Accomodation of Social Change*, Boulder, Westview Press.

Udovitch, Abraham, 1970, *Partnership and Profit in Medieval Islam*, Princeton, Princeton University Press.

————, 1975, 'Refelection on the Institutions of Credit and Banking in the Medieval Islamic Near East', *Studia Islamica*, 1941.

Vatikiotis, P.J., 1987, *Islam and the State*, London, Croom Helm.

Veseth, Michael, 1982, 'The Economics of Property Rights and Human Rights', *American Journal of Economics and Sociology*, 41.

Wallerstein, Immanual, 1974, *The Modern World System*, New York, Academic Press.

————, 1980, *The Modern World System II*, New York, Academic Press.

Wiles, Peter, 1984, 'Epilogue: The Role of Theory', in Wiles, Peter and Routh, Guy, eds., *Economics in Disarray*, Oxford, Basil Blackwell.

Wilson, Peter W., 1991, *A Question of Interest: The Paralysis of Saudi Banking*, Boulder, Westview Press.

Wilson, Rodney, 1990, ed., *Islamic Financial Markets*, London, Routledge.

World Bank, 1992, *Governance and Development*, Washington, D.C. The World Bank.

Nichols Jr., James H., and Wright, Colin, eds., *From Political Economy to Economics, And Back*, San Francisco, Institute of Contemporary Studies.

Zakaria, Rafique, 1989, *The Struggle Within Islam: the Conflict Between Religion and Politics*, London, Penguin.

Zubaida, Sami, 1972, 'Economic and Political Activism in Islam', *Economy and Society*, 1:3, August.

————, 1986, *Islam, the People and the State: Essays on Political Ideas and Movements in the Middle East*, London, Routledge.

INDEX